TORRES STRAIT

• *Thursday Is*

GULF OF
CARPENTARIA

Lizard Is

○ Cooktown

• Cairns
Green Is

CORAL SEA

Great Barrier Reef

PACIFIC OCEAN

Townsville
Bowen

*Swain
Reefs*

Mackay

Rockhampton

Heron Is

QUEENSLAND

Gladstone

Fraser Is

○ BRISBANE

Byron Bay

Coffs Harbour

NEW SOUTH WALES

ADELAIDE

Port Stephens

SYDNEY

Jervis Bay

Kangaroo Is

VICTORIA

TASMAN SEA

Mt Gambier

Eden

MELBOURNE

Pt Fairy

Mallacoota

King Is

BASS
STRAIT

Flinders Is

TASMANIA

HOBART

TORY

TRALIA

una

ncoln

AUSTRALIAN SEA FISHES

NORTH OF 30°S

WTG

AUSTRALIAN
SEA FISHES
NORTH OF 30°S
NEVILLE COLEMAN

DOUBLEDAY
SYDNEY   AUCKLAND   NEW YORK   TORONTO

Also by Neville Coleman

Australian Marine Fishes in Colour
What Shell is That?
Shell Collecting in Australia
Shells in Australia
A Look at Wildlife on the Great Barrier Reef
Australian Fisherman's Fish Guide
Scuba Diver's Introduction to Marine Biology
Field Guide to Australian Marine Life
The Australian Beachcomber
Australian Sea Fishes South of 30°S
Shells Alive!
Field Guide to the Marine Life of S.E. Australia
Fisherman's Catchbook
Fishes of Victoria
Fishes of NSW
Harmful Fishes of Australia
Young Observer's Book of Australian Shells
Guide to Underwater Marine Biology
Nudibranchs of Australasia (co-author R. C. Willan)
Poetry in Pictures – Great Barrier Reef (co-author M. O'Connor)
Guide to Beachcombing
Guide to Seashelling
Australia's Great Barrier Reef (co-authors McLeod & Howes)

AUSTRALIAN SEA FISHES NORTH OF 30°S

First published in 1981 by
Doubleday Australia Pty. Limited

Reprinted in 1988 by Doubleday, a
division of Transworld Publishers
(Aust.) Pty Ltd 15-23 Helles Avenue,
Moorebank NSW 2170

National Library of Australia
Cataloguing-in-Publication Data.

Coleman, Neville
  Australian Sea Fishes North of 30°

  Rev. ed.
  Previous ed.: Sydney: Doubleday, 1981.
  Includes index.
  ISBN 0 86824 115 6.

  1. Marine fishes – Australia I. Title.

597.0994

Typeset by Rochester Photosetting Service, Sydney
Designed by Jim Paton
Printed in Singapore
by Kyodo-Shing Loong Printing Industries Pte. Ltd.

For Rolly McKay

CONTENTS

ACKNOWLEDGMENTS

Many people have contributed in some way to the discovery, description and classification of every species illustrated and described in this book. I cannot know those people, but I can thank them, for without their endeavours my aspirations might, once again, never have been realised.

The photographs in this book are from the files of the Australasian Marine Photographic Index (AMPI). This is an index of colour transparencies showing living animals and plants, cross-referenced against identified specimens housed in musuems and scientific institutes. It also covers related marine activities.

As Curator of the Index, I hope that one day the marine flora and fauna of Australia may be identified alive; if they are, large collections of animals will no longer need to be made for the purposes of identification. If we are to find methods of protecting our seas and husbanding the animals and plants that are in them, people must first be made aware that they exist. It is for this purpose that the AMPI was created.

Although the project is recognised worldwide and is being used by many overseas museums and scientific institutes, as well as by most major museums in Australia, it cannot survive without the co-operation of groups and individuals. The following institutions, societies, companies and individuals have aided the AMPI. Their foresight, interest and assistance will enable the Index to continue its programme of advancing the knowledge of living Australian marine organisms:

Australian Museum; Queensland Museum; New South Wales State Fisheries; National Museum of Victoria; Doubleday Australia Pty Limited; Sea Australia Productions; Jim Tobin, Portland, Oregon (USA); Western Australian Museum; Dr Barry Wilson.

To the trustees of the following institutions and the curators and assistants who have given their time in the identification of specimens and the housing of AMPI collections, I acknowledge my unreserved gratitude:

Australian Museum; Queensland and Western Australian Museums; Dr Gerry Allan; Dianne Blake; Dr Howard Choat (NZ); Dr Doug Hoese; Barry Hutchins; Helen Larson; Rolly McKay; Dr Jack Randall (USA); Dr Barry Russell; Dr Les Knapp (USA); Dr C.E. Dawson (USA); Johann Bell; Dr Dave Pollard.

Once again I am in debt to Rolly McKay, Curator of Fishes at the Queensland Museum, for providing information and constructive advice on the manuscript and insights from his own experience, without which this book would not have succeeded in its high standards.

To Eve and Bill Currie, Aileen and Milton East, Bob and Dinah Halstead, Alison and Rudie Kuiter, Gordon la Praik, Allan Power, Harley Roberts, and Jan and Walter Stark, many thanks for your assistance through the years. To my typists and index compilers, Jan Handley, Jenny Mines and Karen Handley, I am especially grateful.

I also wish to express my gratitude to all the divers, fishermen, aquarists, naturalists, photographers and AMPI explorers who have given of themselves along the way, I sincerely hope my effort is worthy of yours.

Neville Coleman, (IAP)
Curator.

INTRODUCTION

Fish predate man by over 400 million years, and all other vertebrate animals by about 100 million years. As the most ancient vertebrates known, they are ancestors of man and many of our anatomical structures were present in those early fishes.

For those people who may feel a little disconcerted at being related to a mudskipper, or a pufferfish, there is some consolation in the fact that fishes are only very distant relatives. Man has tended to forget that, as a species, he is part and parcel of his environment and, in some way, every living creature on this planet is a part of man and he of it.

The first fishes evolved in the Ordovician period and were armoured, bony creatures without true jaws. They existed by straining organic sediment from the sea floor and deriving nourishment from it.

From these ancient bottom dwellers, fish diversified into many different sizes, shapes and forms. Fish are by far the most successful vertebrates and have established themselves in almost every aquatic niche available. Today there are around 20 000 species thought to exist in the waters of the earth.

Australia has in the vicinity of 3000 species of marine fishes. The correct number may never be known, as new species and new records are being published continuously. Many regions are still unexplored ichthyologically. However, 3000 is an appreciable number when one considers that Australian birds number between 720 and 750 recorded species which have been photographically recorded over the last 70 years.

In many ways it is the very numbers of fish species which have hampered the publication and compilation of knowledge of Australian fishes. Numbers, and the fact that they live in an aquatic environment, which makes observation, collection and photography difficult.

Studies made on the behaviour and mating habits of some birds may be accomplished by setting up a hide at the nest. Very few fishes build nests, most mate just on dusk, or at night, and may do so on the bottom, or near the surface, or in a water column, deep in the ocean.

Most fish shed their reproductive products and it's all over in seconds. To study the young, the eggs must be collected and raised in aquaria, or gathered from the water in plankton nets and identified.

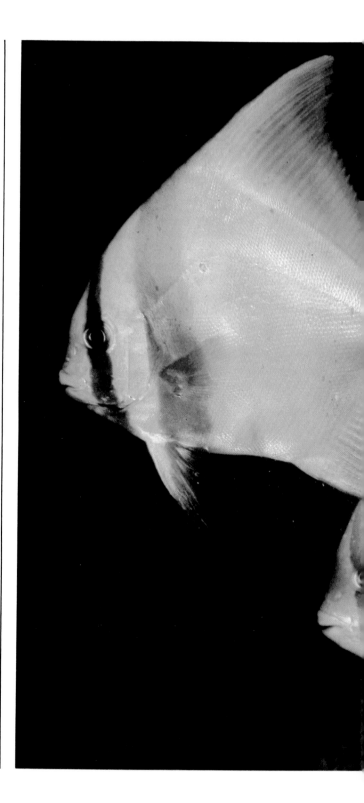

The study of larval fishes is the domain of the specialist as many different species may be caught at the one time.

Is it any wonder that we have a long way to go in recording the life cycles and natural history of our marine fishes considering that it is only some 15 years since we first ventured underwater and began the slow process of learning?

Despite the knowledge gathered by those few people who have studied Australian marine fishes, apart from the scientific names, we know almost nothing about them.

Australia is a recently settled country and our oceans are virtually unsurveyed. Facilities for marine research are only now being implemented and it will take many years of scientific research before we fully document our fish fauna.

If we had one trained ichthyologist for every species of marine fish, it would take many years to gather sufficient data to describe the life history of each fish. We do not have 3000 ichthyologists, nor do we have 300, or even 30. However, with enough field guides providing for the identification of fishes, the amateur ichthyologist can assist in recording the distribution of fishes by sending information, photographs, and specimens to museums. Many new species and new records for Australia have resulted from the interests and efforts of fishermen, underwater naturalists, photographers, beachcombers and students. The complacent attitudes towards marine science and natural history exploration are changing after many years of neglect, and it's about time we all became aware of our responsibilities as a nation towards our seas.

In contrast with its companion volume, *Australian Sea Fishes South 30°S,* this book deals with fishes inhabiting our northern seas. This area has attracted the most scientific study, especially the north-eastern coast and the Great Barrier Reef, and therefore a little more is known of this region. Also, due to popular appeal, it has stimulated many natural history publications. The Great Barrier Reef has had more books written on it than any other part of Australia. Amongst these have been several fish books, most of which have the fishes illustrated in black and white or in colour paintings. More recently, Queensland Government sponsorship has produced an excellent publication issued by the Department of Harbours and Marine, which also includes many photographic studies.

However, there has been very little published on Northern Territory fishes, or on the fishes of north-western Australia, even though many of the east coast species inhabit these areas.

In the area covered by this book there are approximately 2400 species of marine fishes and some yet to be described.

It is not yet feasible to produce a single publication which covers all these species. Nor is it feasible to produce a book featuring all those we do have photographed in colour, as the price would be far too high. This book includes almost 300 photographic studies of living sea fishes, many of which appear here for the first time.

ABOUT THIS BOOK

The fishes selected for this book are based on species living north of an imaginary line drawn across Australia from Houtman Abrolhos in Western Australia to Coff's Harbour in New South Wales. This includes all offshore islands adjacent to those states, which are regarded as part of those states. All species distribution are contained within this area.

Wherever fishes occur in states that do not come into this area, the information is found with the distribution data in brackets.

Map references are only indications that the species has been recorded in that state. No attempt has been made to show specific intrastate distributions, even when these are known. The present situation regarding the geographical ranges of many species is far from well-established, and may remain so for many years.

In writing this book, I have assumed a certain amount of commonsense on the part of the reader. We are all painfully aware that fish have spines which, if not handled with care, can cause unpleasant wounds. However, the label 'dangerous' is only used for fish that could cause injury. 'Venomous' includes all species that have venom glands and 'poisonous' refers to those which, if eaten, cause illness or death.

Number references (e.g. Labrid. No. 40 AMPI) made to animals without specific names are catalogue numbers of specimens contained within the system of the AMPI. In this way, they can be identified in collections and referred to in the future AMPI publications, for the reader's benefit.

PHOTOGRAPHIC DETAILS

Cameras: Hasselblad — 50mm lens — 120mm lens
Rollei Marine — 80mm lens — N°3 diopters
Nikon — 55mm Micro nikkor — 105mm Micro nikkor — 24mm
Nikonos II — 35mm lens — Nikonos III — 15mm lens

Flashes: Metz — 108 — 302B — 402

Film: Kodachrome 64ASA
Ektachrome 64ASA — 200ASA

EXTERNAL BODY FEATURES OF AN ELASMOBRANCH (SHARK)

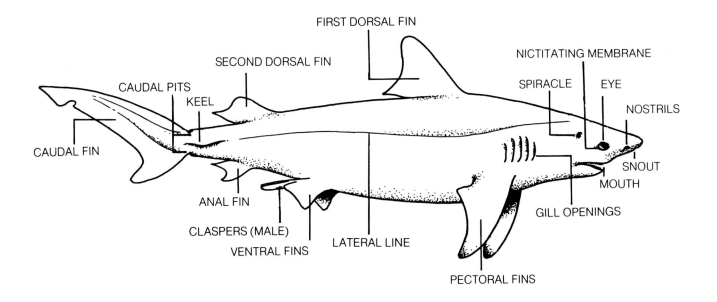

FIRST DORSAL FIN

SECOND DORSAL FIN

NICTITATING MEMBRANE

CAUDAL PITS

SPIRACLE   EYE

KEEL

NOSTRILS

CAUDAL FIN

SNOUT

MOUTH

ANAL FIN

GILL OPENINGS

CLASPERS (MALE)

VENTRAL FINS   LATERAL LINE

PECTORAL FINS

The elasmobranchs are among the most primitive fishes and have changed little in the past 200 million years. They have five to seven pairs of gill openings and no 'bones' but instead are supported internally by flexible cartilage or gristle and externally by a rough scaleless skin in which millions of minute denticles are embedded. They are a very successful group and are found from low tide level down to many thousands of metres.

Because of their voracious appetites and efficient predatory senses, many of the larger sharks have long been feared by man. Australia has a history of shark attacks on humans and this has no doubt helped delay underwater exploration by diving.

13

Family ORECTOLOBIDAE
Common Name Epaulette shark
Scientific Name *Hemiscyllium ocellatum* (Bonaterre), 1788
Habitat Coral reef, lagoons
Distribution Qld., NT, WA
Depth Range Low tide to 10 metres
Adult Size 1 metre
Food Habit Carnivorous: molluscs, worms, crustaceans
Use Edible, but not generally eaten
Occurrence Common

Like many other ground sharks, this easily-identifiable species is a nocturnal forager. It is often seen in shallow water lagoonal areas and amongst scattered reef.

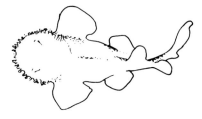

Most specimens observed are in fairly shallow waters and during the day they 'hole' up beneath coral slabs, under ledges and rocks. Despite their sleepy behaviour and placid nature, if held, they show quite an amazing display of strength and dogged tenacity in getting away. Epaulette sharks do not have very good eyesight and rely on their sense of smell and sensory papillae under the snout to detect food. After mating takes place during late winter and summer, the female lays a number of brown horny egg-cases.

Epaulette shark *(H. ocellatum)*, female

Family ORECTOLOBIDAE
Common Name Tasselled wobbegong
Scientific Name *Orectolobus ogilbyi* (Regan), 1909
Habitat Coral reef
Distribution Qld., NT, WA
Depth Range 2 to 40 metres
Adult Size 1.83 metres
Food Habit Carnivorous: fish, crustaceans
Use Edible
Occurrence Moderately common

With its thick squat body, short tail, extensively-branched appendages around the mouth and its characteristic patterning, *O. ogilbyi* is fairly simple to identify. Although there is some variation in colour throughout its range, the whitish-yellow ones seem to be in deep water and the dark browner ones in shallow water. They are frequently found lying under coral ledges during the daytime. These sharks are not aggressive but as they have sharp teeth and a tenacious bite they should not be approached too closely.

Tasselled wobbegong *(O. ogilbyi)*, female

Family ORECTOLOBIDAE
Common Name Leopard shark
Scientific Name *Stegostoma fasciatum* (Hermann), 1783
Habitat Coral reef, rocky reef, sea grass beds, sand
Distribution Qld., NT, WA (also NSW)
Depth Range 2 to 25 metres
Adult Size 2.5 metres
Food Habit Carnivorous: molluscs, crustaceans, fish
Use Edible, but not generally eaten
Occurrence Moderately common

Unlike some other Australian ground sharks, *S. fasciatum* is not likely to be misidentified even by the novice diver. Its blunt head, dorsal keels and long caudal fin, together with its large paddle-like pectorals and colour pattern are characteristic.

This species has been referred to as the zebra shark, but this name only represents small juveniles which are black, or dark purple, with white stripes. Although faint stripes do show on the body of some semi-adults, these fade with age. Leopard sharks are slow and awkward swimmers and during the day they lay on the bottom asleep. Feeding generally occurs at night.

Leopard shark *(S. fasciatum),* female

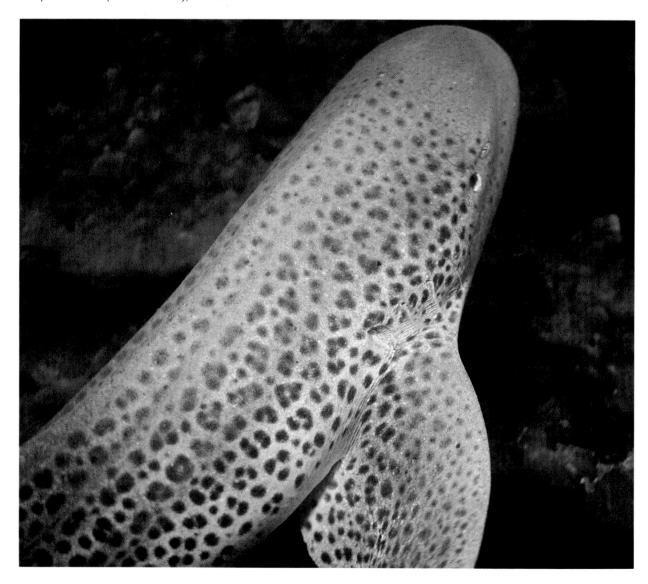

Family TRIAKIDAE
Common Name White-tipped reef shark
Scientific Name *Triaenodon obesus* (Ruppell), 1835
Habitat Coral reef, rocky reef
Distribution Qld., NT, WA (also NSW)
Depth Range 1 to 40 metres
Adult Size 2.3 metres
Food Habit Carnivorous: fish, crustaceans, reptiles
Use Edible, but not generally eaten
Occurrence Common

Found on inshore and offshore reefs throughout northern Australia, *T. obesus* is a slender bodied shark.

Although it has formidable teeth and may be a little pugnacious during feeding frenzies, or in the presence of speared fish, it is generally fairly placid and doesn't trouble divers unduly. It will take hooked fish from lines but isn't quite as much trouble as the gray reef shark. Unlike many pelagic sharks, *T. obesus* does not need to swim continuously to keep water flowing over its gills. I first observed *T. obesus* on the bottom using muscular gill movement for breathing in 1971 in north Western Australia and since then have observed it regularly. This species bears living young.

White-tipped reef shark *(T. obesus)*, female

Family CARCHARHINIDAE
Common Name Galapagos shark
Scientific Name *Carcharhinus galapagensis* (Snodgrass and Heller), 1905
Habitat Coral reef, rocky reef, open ocean
Distribution Qld., NT, WA (also NSW)
Depth Range 5 to 60 metres
Adult Size 3 metres
Food Habit Carnivorous: fish
Use Edible
Occurrence Common

Although the Galapagos shark is somewhat similar in many ways to the gray shark it can be distinguished by its rounder head and fuller body towards the tail. The gray shark is far more sturdy in the front half of the body and is rather steeply angled up to the base of the dorsal fin with a slimmer profile towards the tail.

The Galapagos shark has no keels on the caudal peduncle, though a dermal ridge is present on the back between the fins. Its upper teeth are broadly triangular and serrated, the lower ones are narrower.

In the water, *C. galapagensis* generally swims in schools, it is extremely cheeky and isn't easily scared. Although there are no reported fatalities in Australian seas, I know a few divers who don't mind being bluffed out of the water by these fast, sleek beauties.

Galapagos shark *(C. galapagensis)*, female

Family CARCHARHINIDAE
Common Name Graceful whaler shark, Gray reef shark
Scientific Name *Carcharhinus amblyrhynchos* (Bleeker), 1856
Habitat Coral reef, rocky reef
Distribution Qld., NT, WA (also NSW)
Depth Range 8 to 40 metres
Adult Size 2 metres
Food Habit Carnivorous: fish, turtles, crustaceans
Use Edible (flake)
Occurrence Common

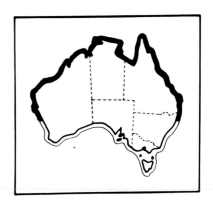

A sleek inquisitive species, the Gray reef shark is a swift efficient predator which occurs mostly on offshore reefs. Although at some locations it may be only sighted occasionally and does not appear to give divers much trouble, in other areas it is quite pugnacious and when there are 20 or 30 around, the fact that they are only 'little ones' doesn't instill much confidence. The Gray reef shark is thick-bodied with a somewhat depressed head, a gray back, white belly and black margins to the pelvic and caudal fins, the ventral tips of the pectorals are also black. This species gives birth to living young.

Graceful whaler shark *(C. amblyrhynchos),* female

Family CARCHARHINIDAE
Common Name Tiger shark
Scientific Name *Galeocerdo cuvieri* (Peron and Le Sueur), 1822
Habitat Open sea, coral reef, rocky reef
Distribution Qld., NT, WA (also NSW)
Depth Range Surface to 40 metres
Adult Size 6 metres
Food Habit Carnivorous: fish, mammals, birds, reptiles
Use Edible
Occurrence Common

A large thick-bodied shark, *G. cuvieri* has a blunt head, a dark greying brown back and is off-white on the belly. Younger sharks have distinct dark stripes on the back which are faded on specimens over 4 metres. The teeth are very characteristic and are coarsely serrated, curved to the side, and identical in both jaws.

Known worldwide as a proven man-eater, the tiger shark is a cosmopolitan species which inhabits the world's major tropical and some temperate seas. Having had fairly close contact and a little time to watch this shark in action on several occasions, I always have the impression of a big slow-moving vacuum cleaner that just moves in, quite casually, and engulfs its food in massive gulps.

Under normal conditions the shark never seems to move fast, unless it has been frightened, or otherwise triggered into an attack pattern by some action. Even a tiger shark's feeding frenzy is performed at what seems a much slower pace than that of smaller sharks. I think that more than anything else the sheer size and destructive dentition is enough to make it one of the oceans greatest scavenging predators.

Tiger shark *(G. cuvieri)* female

Family RHYNCHOBATIDAE
Common Name White-spotted shovelnose ray
Scientific Name *Rhynchobatus djiddensis* Forsskål, 1775
Habitat Sandy lagoons
Distribution Qld., NT, WA
Depth Range 1 to 30 metres
Adult Size 3 metres
Food Habit Carnivorous: fish, molluscs, crustaceans
Use Edible
Occurrence Common

The largest shovelnose ray in Australian waters, this fish possibly grows larger in Western Australian waters and could well reach a size of over 3 metres. While smaller specimens may be light brown in colour with prominent white spots along the sides, large adults tend to be black on the back with white under surface. The two dorsals and caudal fin are light gray on the leading edges and darker on the trailing edges. There is a very prominently noduled dermal ridge on the back between the fins and also around the eyes. This ridge is white, as are the edges to all the fins and body.

They are caught by handlines, in set nets, trawled, speared, and have quite acceptable flesh.

White-spotted shovelnose ray *(R. djiddensis),* female

21

Family DASYATIDAE
Common Name Blue-spotted stingray
Scientific Name *Amphotistius kuhlii* (Muller and Henle), 1841
Habitat Rubble, sand, coral reef, rocky reef
Distribution Qld., NT, WA (also NSW)
Depth Range 8 to 50 metres
Adult Size 38 centimetres
Food Habit Carnivorous: molluscs, crustaceans, fish
Use Edible
Occurrence Common

Not as common as the blue-spotted fantail ray, *A. kuhlii* generally inhabits deeper waters in lagoons and along the bases of underwater cliffs and the slopes of estuarine channels.

It is easily distinguished from the blue-spotted fantail ray by its triangular disc. The blue spots on *A. kuhlii* are not as bright as those on *T. lymna* and are apt to fade once the fish is dead. There are, however, a number of black spots on the back which are very prominent and stable.

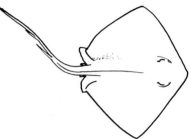

When swimming, *A. kuhlii* holds its tail up high; it is a very nervous little ray and not easy to approach. Specimens are caught by line and numbers also come up in trawls.

Blue-spotted stingray *(A. kuhlii), female*

Family DASYATIDAE
Common Name Mangrove stingray
Scientific Name *Himantura granulata* (Macleay), 1883
Habitat Mangroves, coral reef, mud, sand
Distribution Qld. (also NSW)
Depth Range 1 to 25 metres
Adult Size 1.5 metres
Food Habit Carnivorous: molluscs, fish
Use Edible
Occurrence Common

The Mangrove stingray has the longest tail in comparison to its body of any Australian stingray; this tail may be twice the length of the disc. It occurs on mainland reefs and estuaries and may also be found in upper river systems where it can be caught on handlines and enmeshed in nets. Mangrove stingrays are common around offshore islands and reefs even as far out as Lord Howe Island, where their presence was recorded for the first time in 1980. They have been seen in groups numbering from four to ten specimens. When approached underwater they are a bit skittish and generally move away if disturbed.

Like most smaller stingrays, the skinned flaps of this species are edible. The tail is also an interesting curio, as it has a row of spiny nodules running along its full length.

Mangrove stingray *(H. granulata),* female

Family DASYATIDAE
Common Name Long-tailed ray
Scientific Name *Himantura uarnak* (Forsskål), 1775
Habitat Mud, muddy reef, sand
Distribution Qld., NT, WA (also NSW)
Depth Range 8 centimetres to 20 metres
Adult Size 1.75 metres
Food Habit Carnivorous: molluscs, crustaceans
Use Edible
Occurrence Common

One of the larger tropical stingrays, *H. uarnak* is commonly encountered at mainland and offshore locations and is often seen in large congregations. In many estuaries throughout its range and in particular in sheltered sandy or muddy bays in north Western Australia, this stingray comes into the shallows to sleep, rest, or sun. It may reach a size of 1.75 metres across the disc and it has a continuous mesh-like pattern on the back. The tail has around 35 bands and a single venomous spine. At the centre of the back, along the dorsal ridge there are two prominent white tubercles. The long-tailed ray is sometimes caught on handlines and in trawls.

Long-tailed ray *(H. uarnak)*, female

Family DASYATIDAE
Common Name Blue-spotted fantail ray
Scientific Name *Taeniura lymna* (Forsskål), 1775
Habitat Sand, mud, coral reef, rubble
Distribution Qld., NT, WA (also NSW)
Depth Range 8 centimetres to 20 metres
Adult Size 2.5 metres
Food Habit Carnivorous: molluscs, worms, crustaceans
Use Edible
Occurrence Common

Although this stingray is recorded to reach a size up to some 2.5 metres, very few people would have ever encountered such a large specimen.

On late afternoons, blue-spotted fantail rays are very commonly seen on lagoon floors and tidal flats, where they follow the rising tide searching for molluscs which are crushed by their powerful teeth and jaws.

During the middle of the day they can be found beneath ledges, coral slabs and in caves. These rays are not easily approached underwater and seem to be extremely nervous, always seeking a speedy escape. They are fairly simple to identify, as their oval body shape and brilliant spots are unlike any other ray. The tail has one, or two, venomous spines situated towards the blue tip.

Blue-spotted fantail ray *(T. lymna),* male

25

Family DASYATIDAE
Common Name Black-spotted stingray
Scientific Name *Taeniura melanospilos* (Bleeker), 1853
Habitat Mud, muddy reef, sand
Distribution Qld., (also NSW)
Depth Range 5 to 120 metres
Adult Size 3 metres
Food Habit Carnivorous: molluscs, crustaceans, fish
Use Edible
Occurrence Common

Looking for all the world like an interplanetary space ship, this giant stingray glides along in the depths and when one swims beside it there is an overpowering sense of wonder at being so close to such a large creature.

Seeing such a powerful, majestic animal wild and free in its environment, we must pity the so called 'hunter' who kills it just for 'the sake of' doing so.

This stingray seems to be more common around offshore islands and cays and is often followed around by schools of yellowtail kingfish. Observations have shown that a smaller individual of undetermined species may 'ride' on its back and also lay on it when it is on the bottom.

Black-spotted stingray *(T. melanospilos)* female

Family MOBULIDAE
Common Name Manta ray
Scientific Name *Manta alfredi* (Krefft), 1868
Habitat Oceanic, mid water column
Distribution Qld., NT, WA (also NSW)
Depth Range Surface to 20 metres
Adult Size 5.75 metres
Food Habit Carnivorous: plankton
Use Not generally eaten
Occurrence Moderately common

Harmless giants which in many regions are still referred to as devilfish, manta rays are really gentle creatures that will often endure the clumsy approaches of underwater man and allow themselves to be touched or ridden. Manta rays are usually encountered in pairs, or small groups, although I have swum with up to a dozen of these giants some 10 kilometres off North West Cape in Western Australia, just on dusk — an extremely exhilarating experience.

Food is sieved directly from the water and is comprised of all manner of planktonic organisms. The young are born alive and come out of the mother's body wrapped up in their wingflaps. These soon unfold and may measure 1 metre across; young mantas are called pups.

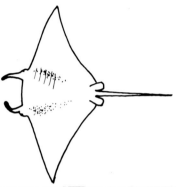

Manta ray *(M. alfredi)*

EXTERNAL BODY FEATURES OF A TELEOST (BONY FISH)

To this class belong all the modern fishes with true bony skeletons. They possess one gill opening on each side and most have an outer covering of scales. Their size ranges from gobies a few millimetres in length to giant gropers and cod measuring up to three metres. These fishes can be carnivorous, herbivorous or omnivorous and feed on a large variety of crustaceans and other fishes. The teleostomes comprise the bulk of edible fish caught in Australia and are extremely diverse in their shapes and colours and in the habitats they occupy.

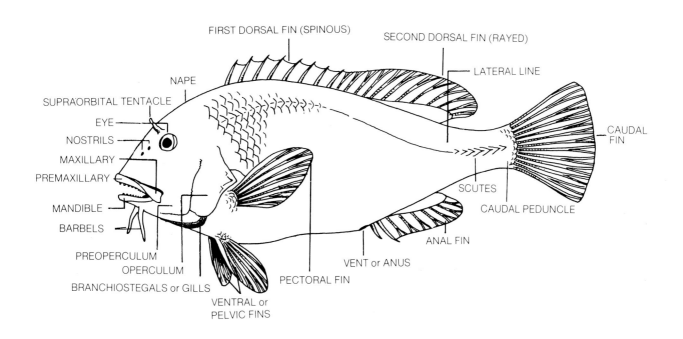

FIRST DORSAL FIN (SPINOUS)

SECOND DORSAL FIN (RAYED)

LATERAL LINE

NAPE

SUPRAORBITAL TENTACLE

EYE

NOSTRILS

MAXILLARY

PREMAXILLARY

MANDIBLE

BARBELS

PREOPERCULUM

OPERCULUM

BRANCHIOSTEGALS or GILLS

VENTRAL or
PELVIC FINS

PECTORAL FIN

VENT or ANUS

ANAL FIN

SCUTES

CAUDAL PEDUNCLE

CAUDAL
FIN

29

Family MURAENIDAE
Common Name Abbott's moray
Scientific Name *Gymnothorax eurostus* (Abbott), 1861
Habitat Coral reef, rocky reef
Distribution Qld. (also NSW)
Depth Range 5 to 10 metres
Adult Size 1 metre
Food Habit Carnivorous: fish, crustaceans
Use Non-edible
Occurrence Uncommon

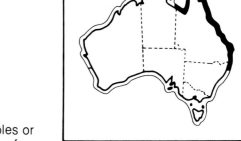

Rarely seen in the open, this moray eel is generally found in holes or beneath coral ledges on offshore islands and reefs. Very few specimens have been collected.

The black tail with its bright yellow spots, is in direct contrast with the front half of the body which has much more prominent yellow markings.

As with other moray eels, the flesh of this species should never be eaten as it could well be poisonous. Divers will find this moray to be rather shy.

Abbott's moray *(G. eurostus)*

Family MURAENIDAE
Common Name Tessellated moray
Scientific Name *Gymnothorax favagineus* Bloch and Schneider, 1801
Habitat Rocky reef, coral reef
Distribution Qld., NT, WA
Depth Range 2 to 25 metres
Adult Size 1 metre
Food Habit Carnivorous: fish, crustaceans, molluscs
Use Non-edible
Occurrence Uncommon

The tessellated moray is an easily identified tropical moray which is more frequently seen on offshore island and reefs than on the mainland. On the Great Barrier Reef these eels are often seen by fossickers wading back through shallow lagoons after a day out on the reef flats. This eels will not attack waders, for morays are not as aggressive as some would have us think. I have swum with morays well over two metres in length, that will take food from your hand as gently as a baby, and even come out of the coral and wrap themselves around you while looking for more food. However, each one should be treated with respect until such time as it becomes familiar with its benefactor.

Tessellated moray *(G. favagineus)*

Family OPHICHTHYIDAE
Common Name Banded snake eel
Scientific Name *Leiuranus semicinctus* (Lay and Bennett), 1839
Habitat Sand, sea grass meadows
Distribution Qld. (also NSW)
Depth Range 1 to 10 metres
Adult Size 50 centimetres
Food Habit Carnivorous
Use Non-edible
Occurrence Uncommon

Snake eels are delightfully interesting fishes that inhabit sandy lagoons and harbours in both inshore and offshore areas.

Although most are nocturnal, some individuals may be seen on overcast days, or around dusk, foraging out in the open in search of food. The banded snake eel has an extremely good sense of smell and when searching for food it slides slowly along the bottom inserting its nose into the sand as it goes. In this way, it apparently picks up the scent of prey species. Rarely caught on lines and unlikely to be trawled, they are impossible to catch and hold by hand. Invariably, they slip away and burrow tail first into the sand, to be gone in an instant.

Banded snake eel *(L. semicinctus)*

Family SYNODONTIDAE
Common Name Hoult's lizardfish
Scientific Name *Synodus houlti* McCulloch, 1921
Habitat Sand
Distribution Qld., NT, WA
Depth Range 3 to 10 metres
Adult Size 17 centimetres
Food Habit Carnivorous: fish
Use Edible but not generally eaten
Occurrence Common

Due to their cryptic colouration and secretive habits, many lizardfish remain unnoticed by the majority of divers. Some sit on the corals, propped up on their pelvic fins and others bury in the sand and rubble, waiting to ambush small fishes as they swim within range. A few species of lizardfish occur in several types of habitats and some are restricted to one. *S. houlti* appears to be found in areas of sand, or sandy rubble where it partly buries its body in the substrate. It inhabits inshore areas, continental islands and offshore locations throughout its range and is a solitary, diurnal species. Hoult's lizardfish is regularly trawled and sometimes caught by line while on the drift; although edible it is usually regarded as a 'trash fish'.

Hoult's lizardfish *(S. houlti)*

Family SYNODONTIDAE
Common Name Engleman's lizardfish
Scientific Name *Synodus englemani* Schultz, 1953
Habitat Coral reef, rocky reef
Distribution Qld. (also NSW)
Depth Range 3 to 20 metres
Adult Size 20 centimetres
Food Habit Carnivorous: fish
Use Edible but not generally eaten
Occurrence Uncommon

S. englemani is a cryptic ambusher that generally sits, or perches on outcrops of living coral, or in colonies of soft coral, and seems to prefer to be in a semi-vertical position. I have only observed solitary specimens; this species is by no means as common as its relative, *S. variegatus,* (see *Australian Sea Fishes South 30°S*), which has a somewhat similar habitat and behaviour. Engleman's lizardfish is a very attractive little species with a blotched grey and red back, and a line of ten red elongated, rectangular blocks just above the lateral line running from the head down to the caudal peduncle. The dorsal fin has red and white spots on the rays.

Engleman's lizardfish *(S. englemani)*

Family BATRACHOIDIDAE
Common Name Dahl's frogfish
Scientific Name *Batrachomoeus dahli* (Rendahl), 1922
Habitat Rocky reef
Distribution WA
Depth Range 1 to 20 metres
Adult Size 15 centimetres
Food Habit Carnivorous: crustaceans, molluscs, echinoderms, fish
Use Edible
Occurrence Moderately common

Due to its remote location from the rest of Australia, many of the fishes of north Western Australia are only just appearing in modern books. Although Dahl's frogfish was described nearly 60 years ago, this is the first time it has been reproduced in colour.

Dahl's frogfish is very localised in its distribution and is only known from Shark Bay to Broome, occurring along the mainland and on offshore islands adjacent to the coast. This fish inhabits intertidal pools and has also been taken by trawlers.

Like other frogfish, it swallows its food whole and has an extremely large appetite.

Dahl's frogfish *(B. dahli)*

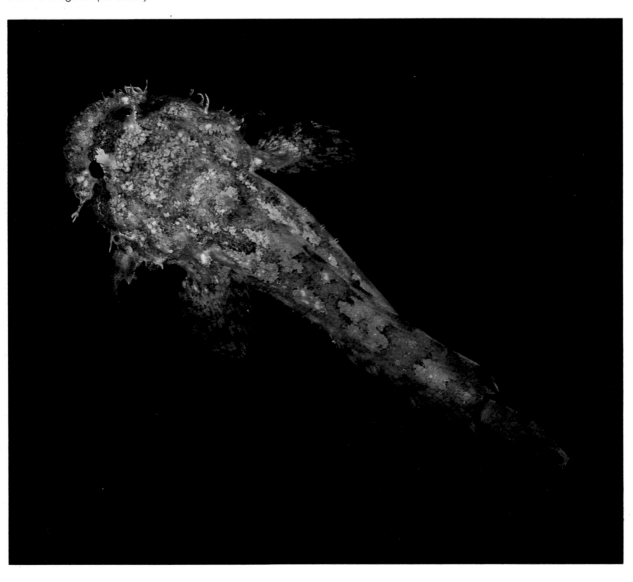

Family BATRACHOIDIDAE
Common Name Australian frogfish
Scientific Name *Halophryne diemensis* (Le Sueur), 1824
Habitat Rocky reef, coral reef, mud
Distribution Qld., NT, WA
Depth Range Intertidal to 20 metres
Adult Size 19 centimetres
Food Habit Carnivorous: crustaceans, molluscs
Use Edible
Occurrence Common

Quite a common species, the Australian frogfish is rarely seen out in the open during the day and is only found by searching in caves, or beneath slabs of coral.

There are three main colour variations in this species, a spotted form in Western Australia and Northern Territory, a non-spotted plain form in Western Australia and a non-spotted ornate patterned form in Northern Territory and Queensland. The range of this species extends from Shark Bay in Western Australia across to Heron Island where I photographed a number in 1974.

Little is known of its breeding habits. Specimens are often brought up by trawlers.

Australian frogfish *(H. diemensis)*

Family ANTENNARIIDAE
Common Name Spot-tailed anglerfish
Scientific Name *Lophiocharon caudimaculatus* (Rüppell), 1835
Habitat Rocky reef, mud, coral reef
Distribution WA, NT
Depth Range 1 to 20 metres
Adult Size 22 centimetres
Food Habit Carnivorous: fish, crustaceans
Use Aquarium fish
Occurrence Moderately common

Anglerfishes are often far more prevalent than the records show, for unless they are collected by fish poison, or are trawled, very few are found without some knowledge of their habitats. Underwater, only a few experienced divers have ever seen more than one or two species.

The spot-tailed anglerfish is one of the largest shallow-water anglerfishes and, despite its size, is difficult to locate, as it resembles the bottom growths to an amazing degree.

Like most anglerfish, it has a gross appetite and attracts its prey towards its mouth by means of a 'fishing rod' and an energetically wriggled 'lure'.

Spot-tailed anglerfish *(L. caudimaculatus)*

Family ANTENNARIIDAE
Common Name Ocellated anglerfish
Scientific Name *Antennarius nummifer* (Cuvier), 1817
Habitat Coral reef, rocky reef, rubble
Distribution Qld., NT, WA
Depth Range 5 to 25 metres
Adult Size 16 centimetres
Food Habit Carnivorous: fish, crustaceans
Use Aquarium fish
Occurrence Uncommon

A very curious little anglerfish which is still fairly rare in most museum collections, *A. nummifer* is resident on mainland reefs and offshore islands and cays where it lives amongst rubble reef on channel slopes and in the vicinity of dead coral patches behind the reef.

It has a rough textured skin with small filaments on it. There are extensive filaments around the lower mouth area and the short fishing rod resembles a small bunch of weed rather than the normal modified dorsal spine of other anglers.

This species has rarely been figured in colour before and although there is some variation within the species, all specimens have an ocellus at the base of the dorsal fin between the seventh and ninth ray.

Ocellated anglerfish *(A. nummifer)*

Family BELONIDAE
Common Name Needlefish
Scientific Name *Platybelone argala platyura* (Bennett), 1832
Habitat Surface waters
Distribution Qld.
Depth Range Surface to 5 metres
Adult Size 50 Centimetres
Food Habit Carnivorous: fish
Use Edible
Occurrence Common

Needlefish seem to be an offshore species found around islands and cays of the Great Barrier Reef and out into the Coral Sea. Like all belonids, they are a gregarious schooling species which patrol the surface waters of lagoons and semi-sheltered waters, feeding on small sprats.

Underwater, they are very shy and with the approach of a diver melt into the distance. They must move very fast when feeding or being chased by larger carnivores as I once found a skull and beak embedded in a floating coconut.

Needlefish *(P. argala platyura)*

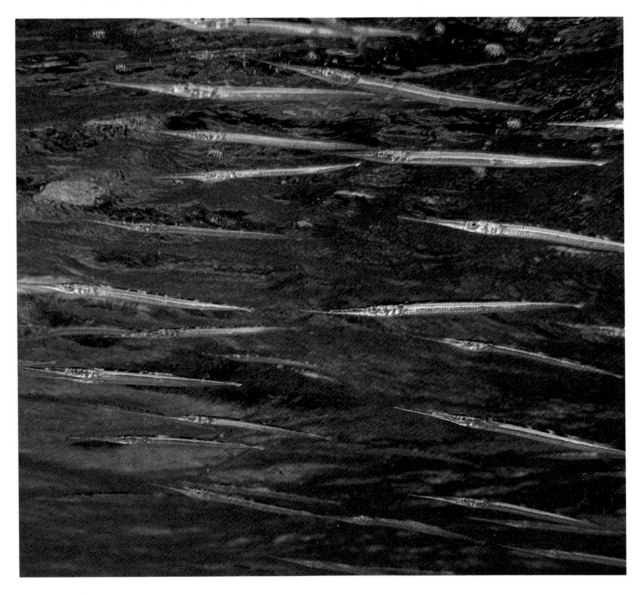

Family HOLOCENTRIDAE
Common Name Horned squirrelfish
Scientific Name *Sargocentron cornutus* Bleeker, 1853
Habitat Coral reef
Distribution Qld.
Depth Range 10 to 20 metres
Adult Size 20 centimetres
Food Habit Carnivorous: fish
Use Edible
Occurrence Uncommon

Although there are around thirteen species of squirrelfishes recorded from Australian waters, this is by no means conclusive, as there may be undescribed species awaiting discovery.

The horned squirrelfish is nocturnal and even on late afternoons it rarely comes out in the open. When it does dart from one hole to another in order to snatch one inquisitive look at an underwater photographer, it doesn't waste time.

The species has a characteristic colour pattern and a large preopercular spine. It is found along the northern Great Barrier Reef and in the Coral Sea.

Horned squirrelfish *(S. cornutus)*

40

Family HOLOCENTRIDAE
Common Name Violet squirrelfish
Scientific Name *Sargocentron violaceus* Bleeker, 1853
Habitat Coral reef
Distribution Qld., WA
Depth Range 5 to 10 metres
Adult Size 22 centimetres
Food Habit Carnivorous: fish, crustaceans
Use Edible
Occurrence Rare

This species was first recorded in north Western Australia and many years passed before it was eventually discovered living on reefs in the Coral Sea.

Specimens have been observed to live in gutters behind the reef ramparts where they inhabit holes and ledges along the sides and lower areas of the gutters. They are very shy during the day and, although their inquisitive nature often gets the better of them, they are not easily photographed in the surging waters breaking over the reef.

Distinguishing features are a red head, violet-barred scales, a red spot on the upper caudal peduncle and a black mark on the upper operculum (gill cover).

Like all other members of this genus there is a very prominent preopercular spine present.

Violet squirrelfish *(S. violaceus)*

Family HOLOCENTRIDAE
Common Name Red squirrelfish
Scientific Name *Sargocentron ruber* (Forsskål), 1775
Habitat Rocky reef, coral reef
Distribution Qld, NT, WA
Depth Range 3 to 20 metres
Adult Size 22 centimetres
Food Habit Carnivorous: fish
Use Edible
Occurrence Common

Found along the length of the Great Barrier Reef and around some inshore and offshore reefs of north Western Australia, the red squirrelfish is probably the best known of the entire squirrelfish family. This is not so surprising as all species are basically nocturnal foraging fishes which spend the daytime in the dark places of the reef. However, a few species, including *S. ruber*, may be seen out of their coral fortresses during overcast days, or during late afternoon when the sun is low. The red squirrelfish often congregates in small groups beneath tabular staghorn corals.

This species has a very long preopercular spine and serrated scales. It feeds on smaller fishes and crustaceans and is sometimes caught on handlines.

Red squirrelfish *(S. ruber)*

Family HOLOCENTRIDAE
Common Name Kuntee squirrelfish
Scientific Name *Myripristis kuntee* Cuvier, 1831
Hatibat Coral reef
Distribution Qld., WA
Depth Range 10 to 25 metres
Adult Size 15 centimetres
Food Habit Carnivorous: fish, crustaceans
Use Edible
Occurrence Uncommon

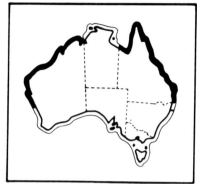

A resident of the Great Barrier Reef's northern area, this rather attractive squirrelfish extends its range far out into the Coral Sea. Rather than live in the upper parts of the reef crest corals as do other species of squirrel-fish, M. kuntee tends to reside along the drop offs and reef slopes which border deeper channels. It is not always easy to approach and will invariably turn to head away from the camera. This results in a poor underwater photograph as the head of *M. kuntee* is quite dark and is often underexposed. In some localities, this species may be common.

Kuntee squirrelfish *(M. kuntee)*

Family HOLOCENTRIDAE
Common Name Red-orange squirrelfish
Scientific Name *Myripristis vittatus* Cuvier, 1831
Habitat Coral reef
Distribution Qld.
Depth Range 10 to 30 metres
Adult Size 14 centimetres
Food Habit Carnivorous: fish
Use Edible
Occurrence Uncommon

Many of the records of Australian squirrelfish have been discovered by the underwater photographers and scientists who have ventured into places off the beaten track to photograph and collect specimens so the fish fauna of an area may be documented. *M. vittatus* has only recently been recorded from Australian waters. A rather beautiful species, it lives in groups along the cliff faces and channel slopes of northern reefs in the Coral Sea. Rather than inhabiting coral, it tends to inhabit holes and caves lower down the reef slope. This is the first colour record of *M. vittatus* to be reproduced in Australia.

Red-orange squirrelfish *(M. vittatus)*

Family AULOSTOMIDAE
Common Name Painted flutemouth
Scientific Name *Aulostoma chinensis* (Linnaeus), 1766
Habitat Coral reef, rocky reef
Distribution Qld., NT, WA (also NSW)
Depth Range 3 to 20 metres
Adult Size 75 centimetres
Food Habit Carnivorous: fish
Use Edible
Occurrence Common

Unlikely to be mistaken for any other species, the painted flutemouth has three main colour phases, bright yellow, grey with white markings, and red with white and black markings. This fish inhabits shallow waters around inshore and offshore reefs where it is an efficient diurnal hunter. Very often *A. chinensis* chooses another fish as a cover to approach schools of small damsels, or other fishes upon which it preys. The cover fish are either herbivores, or large carnivores that only hunt at dawn, or dusk. By choosing this type of cover species, *A. chinensis* is able to approach an unsuspecting prey. Yellow phase *A. chinensis* normally choose yellow cover fish whilst grey phase forms choose dark cover fishes.

Painted flutemouth *(A. chinensis)* Inset: Colour phase

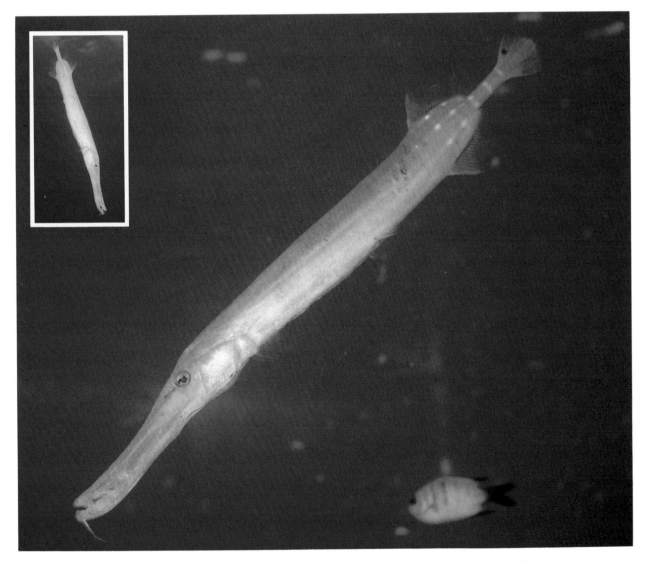

Family SYNGNATHIDAE
Common Name Spotted seahorse
Scientific Name *Hippocampus kuda* Bleeker, 1852
Habitat Rocky reef, sea grass meadows
Distribution Qld. (also NSW)
Depth Range 2 to 30 metres
Adult Size 30 centimetres
Food Habit Carnivorous: crustaceans
Use Aquarium fish
Occurrence Common

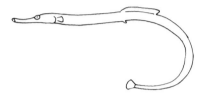

Found on both mainland and offshore reefs, the spotted seahorse may be observed in sheltered estuaries, or along the coast where conditions are fairly stable, such as in bays, or behind groynes.

Although this species is called the spotted seahorse, in life this is not always so, as there are several colour variations, one of which does not have spots. White specimens generally have black spots but these spots do not show on living seahorses of the orange colour phase. Somewhat similar to *H. whitei,* the spotted seahorse can be distinguished by the discontinuation of the central body ridge which does not go below the dorsal fin.

Spotted seahorse *(H. kuda)*

Family SYNGNATHIDAE
Common Name Ladder pipefish
Scientific Name *Festucalex scalaris* (Günther), 1870
Habitat Rocky reefs
Distribution WA
Depth Range 1 to 5 metres
Adult Size 17 centimetres
Food Habit Carnivorous: crustaceans
Use Aquarium fish
Occurrence Moderately common

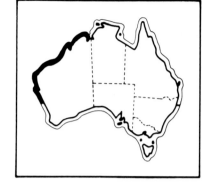

Known for a long time under the genus *Ichthyocampus*, the ladder pipefish has now been placed in the genus *Festucalex* by the world's foremost worker on pipefishes, Dr C. E. Dawson.

Ladder pipefish are residents of mainland rocky-reef where there is an abundance of brown algae. As they are not strong swimmers, they inhabit sheltered lagoons, inlets and bays. Mating takes place in early summer and the females deposit their eggs in the sub-caudal brood pouch of the male who protects the eggs until the tiny pipefishes hatch. Males and females are similar in colour and have 13 to 16 cross-bars down the length of the body.

Ladder pipefish *(F. scalaris)*

Family SYNGNATHIDAE
Common Name Winged pipefish
Scientific Name *Halicampus macrorhynchus* (Randall and Dawson), 1976
Habitat Rubble, coral reef, sand
Distribution Qld., NT
Depth Range 10 to 30 metres
Adult Size 10 centimetres
Food Habit Carnivorous: crustaceans
Use Aquarium fish
Occurrence Rare

A fairly recent entry on the marine faunal lists of Australia, the winged pipefish has been seen by only a handful of people and photographed by even fewer.

It lives on sandy coral rubble bottom at the edges of drop offs and along the slopes of channel entrances through the outer Barrier Reef. As its shape implies, this species has an affinity towards dead pieces of algae which drift, or lie on the bottom, and it is around these that it is mostly found.

I was on the expedition that originally discovered the first one, during a poison station at Lizard Island and years later went back and found them alive. Young ones have very enlarged 'wings', which reduce in size as the animal grows. Adults are quite plain.

Winged pipefish *(H. macrorhynchus)*   Inset: juvenile

Family SCORPAENIDAE
Common Name Ragged-finned scorpionfish
Scientific Name *Pterois antennata* (Bloch), 1787
Habitat Coral reef
Distribution Qld. (also NSW)
Depth Range 8 to 25 metres
Adult Size 25 centimetres
Food Habit Carnivorous: fish, crustaceans
Use Aquarium fish
Occurrence Common

This fish seems to be far more common in the northern areas of the Great Barrier Reef and the Coral Sea than it does in the southern reefs, or mainland island reefs. As with most of its relatives, *P. antennata* is not seen out in the open during the day. It resides beneath ledges and in caves and is generally observed in an upside-down position. Most sightings are of pairs of similar sized fish. Although the fishes of the genus *Pterois* may all look the same, they are really fairly simple to separate with critical observation.

Ragged-finned scorpionfish *(P. antennata)*

Family SCORPAENIDAE
Common Name Fire fish
Scientific Name *Pterois volitans* (Linnaeus), 1758
Habitat Coral reef, rocky reef
Distribution Qld., NT, WA (also NSW)
Depth Range 8 to 40 metres
Adult Size 38 centimetres
Food Habit Carnivorous: fish, crustaceans
Use Aquarium fish
Occurrence Common

Certainly the most common and best known in its genus, *P. volitans* is the favourite of all underwater photographers and many aquarists.

It occupies territories on mainland and offshore reefs and in some areas is extremely common. Juveniles are exquisite and certainly are an excellent fish to observe feeding in aquariums. They are also relatively easy to keep.

Colour ranges from pink to black, the body being crossed with thin pairs of white bands. An easy method by which to separate the species of the genus *Pterois* is to look closely at the pectoral fins, each one has characteristic pectorals regardless of the colours, or geographical location.

Fire fish *(P. volitans)*

Family SCORPAENIDAE
Common Name Butterfly scorpionfish
Scientific Name *Dendrochirus zebra* (Quoy and Gaimard), 1825
Habitat Coral reef, rocky reef, rubble
Distribution Qld., NT, WA (also NSW)
Depth Range 8 to 45 metres
Adult Size 30 centimetres
Food Habit Carnivorous: fish, crustaceans
Use Aquarium fish
Occurrence Common

I have always had a soft spot for *D. zebra* as it was chosen by the publishers as the cover for my first book. Since then I have photographed many others.

Although *D. zebra* resembles other scorpionfish of the genus *Pterois* it can be easily identified by its colour pattern and the shape of its pectoral fin. This fish also differs somewhat from the *Pterois* group in its behaviour. Whereas *P. volitans* is mostly seen with its pectorals extended (even when on the bottom) quite often *D. zebra* is observed hiding amongst bottom growths with its pectorals folded, lying in ambush for unsuspecting prey. In contrast to its slow swimming behaviour, *D. zebra* has an extremely swift hunting strike. Regardless of its venomous spines, the flesh is quite edible.

Butterfly scorpionfish *(D. zebra)*

Family SCORPAENIDAE
Common Name Short-finned scorpionfish
Scientific Name *Dendrochirus brachypterus* (Cuvier), 1829
Habitat Coral reef, rocky reef
Distribution Qld., NT (also NSW)
Depth Range 5 to 40 metres
Adult Size 20 centimetres
Food Habit Carnivorous: fish, crustaceans
Use Aquarium fish
Occurrence Moderately common

Generally inhabiting inshore reefs, *D. brachypterus* is not as commonly encountered as *D. zebra*. The short-finned scorpionfish has the same basic habits as *D. zebra* and is rarely observed swimming in the open. It often lays about in soft corals waiting for small fish to swim past. This species makes a good aquarium pet and can be weaned off live food; although natural feeding is much more desirable, it is at times inconvenient.

The body pattern and the shape of the large pectoral fins are somewhat similar to *D. zebra*. However, *D. brachypterus* can be separated by the broad dark bars on the pectoral.

Short-finned scorpionfish *(D. brachypterus)*

Family SCORPAENIDAE
Common Name Three-spined scorpionfish
Scientific Name *Taenianotus triacanthus* Lacepede, 1802
Habitat Rocky reef, coral reef
Distribution Qld. (also NSW)
Depth Range 5 to 100 metres
Adult Size 12 centimetres
Food Habit Carnivorous: fish, crustaceans
Use Aquarium fish
Occurrence Uncommon

Looking more like an anglerfish than a scorpionfish, *T. triacanthus* is an intriguing little fish which sits and lays around on the bottom behaving for all the world like a leaf, or a piece of algae. Quite often one is seen at the bottom of a small cleft in the coral rock alternately rocking from one side to the other on its pectoral fins. Its camouflage is identical to its surroundings, though most I have seen have been whitish-lemon with specks of red and yellow. Sometimes these fish are not patterned and may be red, yellow, or black. The body of this little fish is quite compressed and the dorsal fin is connected to the tail, which is an unusual feature in scorpaenids.

Three-spined scorpionfish *(T. triacanthus)*

Family SCORPAENIDAE
Common Name Devil scorpionfish
Scientific Name *Scorpaenopsis diabolus* (Cuvier), 1829
Habitat Rocky reef, coral reef, rubble
Distribution Qld., WA, NT (also NSW)
Depth Range 10 to 30 metres
Adult Size 30 centimetres
Food Habit Carnivorous: fish
Use Edible
Occurrence Rare

In all the thousands of hours I have spent in the water around the shores of Australia, I have only observed this fish on a few occasions. Similar in shape to the false stonefish, this exhibits many of the latter fish's habits and behaviour. In the field I use features of the head to separate them. Whereas the head of the false stonefish is covered in soft filaments and appears to be soft, the head of the devil scorpionfish is like that of an armoured skull with a definite separation line between the back of the head and the shoulder hump. The body scales seem more prominent on the devil scorpionfish and with less dermal appendages.

Devil scorpionfish *(S. diabolus)*

Family SCORPAENIDAE
Common Name False stonefish
Scientific Name *Scorpaenopsis gibbosa* (Bloch and Schneider), 1801
Habitat Rocky reef, coral reef, rubble
Distribution Qld., NT, WA
Depth Range 5 to 25 metres
Adult Size 21 centimetres
Food Habit Carnivorous: fish
Use Edible
Occurrence Uncommon

The false stonefish is very often mistaken for the true stonefish and though to the uninitiated these fishes may look similar, there is little similarity in the toxicity of their venom.

Recorded from the inshore and offshore reefs of tropical Australia, this fish inhabits the entire Great Barrier Reef and can be found on broken coral rubble bottom where it sits resembling its habitat. Invariably the false stonefish sits with its head elevated, mouth up, pectorals spread and eyes ever aware. In many circumstances individuals will sit behind rocks or along the sides of coral slabs where their presence is even more camouflaged. Colours are generally green to brownish, mottled with white.

False stonefish (*S. gibbosa*)

Family SCORPAENIDAE
Common Name Horrid stonefish, true stonefish
Scientific Name *Synanceia horrida* (Linnaeus), 1762
Habitat Mud, coral reef, rocky reef, rubble
Distribution Qld., NT, WA
Depth Range 1 to 40 metres
Adult Size 33 centimetres
Food Habit Carnivorous: fish, crustaceans
Use Edible
Occurrence Common

For many years the horrid stonefish was only thought to occur on and around the muddy reefs of mainland estuaries, bays, inlets and lagoons and on the fringing reefs of mainland islands.

Since I photographed this species at Tryon Island on the Great Barrier Reef in 1969 these facts have now been updated, as our knowledge increases it is inevitable that there will be many changes to records now and in the future. The horrid stonefish is one of the most venomous fishes in Australian waters; concealed in dorsal sheaths along the back are thirteen of the most efficient natural injection systems to be found in any marine animal. Needle-sharp spines each with a twin venom sack produce wounds of unbearable pain and the victim must receive medical attention as soon as possible.

Horrid stonefish *(S. horrida)*

Family SCORPAENIDAE
Common Name North-west stonefish
Scientific Name *Dampierosa daruma* Whitley, 1932
Habitat Rocky reef, mud, sand
Distribution WA
Depth Range Intertidal to 30 metres
Adult Size 20 centimetres
Food Habit Carnivorous: fish, crustaceans
Use Edible
Occurrence Rare

Recorded from the north Western Australian mainland and offshore reefs, this little stonefish prefers a sandy mud and rubble rock habitat. Since its initial discovery this fish has only just been reproduced in colour. Recognition is quite straightforward as there are few other fish of similar appearance in Australian waters. It has been taken in seine nets and also comes up in the cod ends of trawlers.

This fish is capable of inflicting a most agonising sting with its dorsal spines. It is still fairly rare in most museum collections.

North-west stonefish *(D. daruma)*

57

Family SCORPAENIDAE
Common Name Merlet's scorpionfish
Scientific Name *Rhinopias aphanes* Eschmeyer, 1973
Habitat Coral reef
Distribution Qld.
Depth Range 10 to 30 metres
Adult Size 23 centimetres
Food Habit Carnivorous: fish
Use Aquarium fish
Occurrence Rare

One of the rarest and most spectacular of the scorpionfishes, *R. aphanes* was first discovered on the outer reefs off New Caledonia, and until 1980 the type species was the only known specimen. In 1980 Dinah Halstead of Tropical Diving Adventures, Port Moresby, Papua New Guinea, found the second fish and it is now known to occur on the Great Barrier Reef, off Townsville.

This fish is readily identified and there is relatively little change in pattern, or colour, throughout its distribution. Extremely difficult to find unless one knows where and what to look for, Merlet's scorpionfish sits out on dead coral outcrops on the slopes of front and back reefs. It is fairly typical in its attitude though it has been noticed to sway from side to side. There is some question as to whether *R. aphanes* may appear to mimic feather stars.

Merlet's scorpionfish *(R. aphanes)*

Family PLATYCEPHALIDAE
Common Name Flag-tail flathead
Scientific Name *Platycephalus arenarius* Ramsay and Ogilby, 1886
Habitat Sand, mud
Distribution Qld., NT (also NSW)
Depth Range 3 to 50 metres
Adult Size 31 centimetres
Food Habit Carnivorous: fish, crustaceans
Use Edible
Occurrence Common

For many years after I began diving I had a rather predetermined concept left over from my old fishing days, that to waste a good flathead by pumping it full of formalin and throwing it into a collecting drum was indeed, sacrilege. So my first collections were just heads. Then I discovered that, for identification, the tails were also important, so I collected both heads and tails. After sixteen years of struggling to make ends meet I must admit, it is easier to identify them from the whole fish.

The flag-tail flathead is generally line caught in mainland estuaries, bays and inlets on prawn bait and has a very characteristic colour pattern on the tail.

Flag-tail flathead *(P. arenarius)*

Family DACTYLOPTERIDAE
Common Name Oriental sea robin
Scientific Name *Dactyloptaena orientalis* (Cuvier and Valenciennes), 1829
Habitat Sand, mud, rubble
Distribution Qld., NT (also NSW)
Depth Range 3 to 40 metres
Adult Size 40 centimetres
Food Habit Carnivorous: crustaceans, worms, molluscs
Use Edible
Occurrence Uncommon

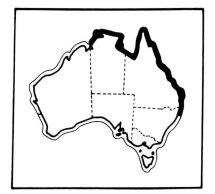

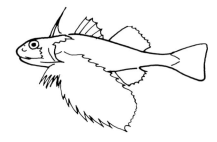

Often referred to in some Australian publications as the flying gurnard, or purple flying gurnard, this fish has little application for flying in air, or even gliding for that matter. Unlike flying fish, its pectorals are neither gossamer thin, nor small enough to enable the fish to even lift them out of the water, let alone reach a speed necessary to glide through air for any distance.

The oriental sea robin is a bottom dwelling fish which occurs at inshore and offshore localities in the vicinity of sand or muddy sea floor. When searching for food, it crawls along the sandy bottom on its modified pelvic fins with its wings folded along the sides and uses the mobile finger-like extensions of its pectoral fins to disturb prey from the sand. This species comes up in trawls and is also line caught.

Family PEGASIDAE
Common Name Short dragonfish
Scientific Name *Eurypegasus draconis* (Linnaeus), 1758
Habitat Sand, rubble
Distribution Qld., WA (also NSW)
Depth Range 3 to 50 metres
Adult Size 7 centimetres
Food Habit Carnivorous: crustaceans
Use Aquarium fish
Occurrence Uncommon

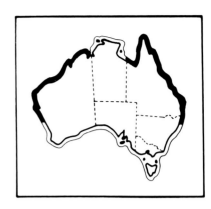

This curious little fish is about as far away from the general shape of fishes, as is possible. More likely to be brought up in the nets of prawn trawlers and research vessels than to be seen on the bottom by a diver, very few *E. draconis* have ever been photographed underwater. To my knowledge only five or six divers on the east coast have ever seen this species on the bottom.

The short dragonfish lives on sandy weed bottom around reef, and on rubble bottom, and is resident in inshore waters as well as offshore waters. There is some indication of sexual dimorphism within this species. Although it crawls around the bottom with its large pectorals extended it doesn't seem to swim very frequently.

Short dragonfish *(E. draconis)*

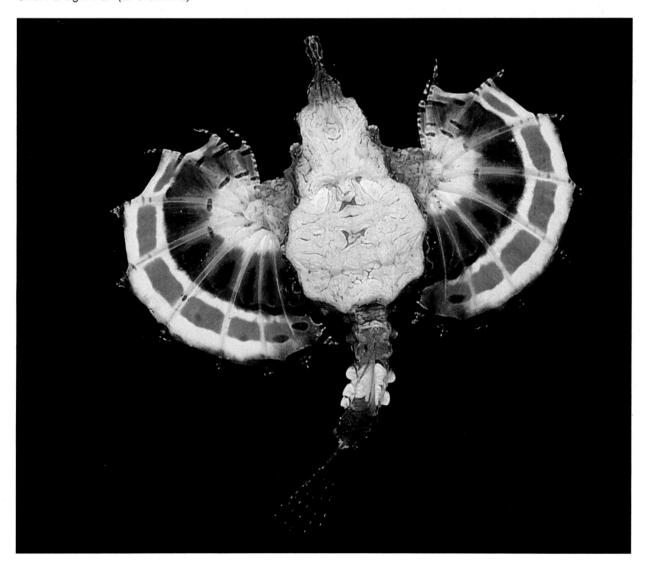

Family CENTROPOMIDAE
Common Name Pink-eyed bass
Scientific Name *Psammoperca waigiensis* (Cuvier), 1828
Habitat Rocky reef, coral reef, sea grass meadows
Distribution Qld., NT, WA
Depth Range 1 to 25 metres
Adult Size 38 centimetres
Food Habit Carnivorous: fish
Use Edible
Occurrence Common

Found throughout tropical Australia, this species inhabits mainland reefs and some closely situated mainland islands where it congregates in small groups. It comes into shallow water during high tide and is often seen in the deep intertidal pools of reefs on the North-West Coast; in these situations it is speared by Aboriginals who for some reason don't seem all that fond of diving for them.

The flesh is white and firm and when fresh is as good as its relative the barramundi. Pink-eyed bass can be separated from barramundi on their colouration which is bronze brown, against the barramundi's green, or grey.

Pink-eyed bass *(P. waigiensis)*

Family SERRANIDAE
Common Name Lunar-tailed rock-cod
Scientific Name *Variola louti* (Forsskål), 1775
Habitat Coral reef, rocky reef
Distribution Qld., NT, WA (also NSW)
Depth Range 5 to 40 metres
Adult Size 76 centimetres
Food Habit Carnivorous: fish, crustaceans
Use Edible
Occurrence Moderately common

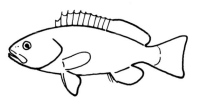

I believe that Australian oceans contain some of the most beautiful fish in the world, many of the serranids being particularly colourful, especially the lunar-tailed rock-cod.

These fish are very shy and in most instances one sees only a fleeting glimpse as the fish melts into the distance at high speed.

The lunar-tailed rock-cod does not appear to be common in any areas I have dived and it is quite a rarity in heavily fished or speared locations. From my first sighting, it took another 12 years to obtain good photographs. Although this species is handlined on fish bait and is sometimes trolled on lures, it feeds largely on coral crabs. I've been told it is extremely good to eat.

Lunar-tailed rock-cod *(V. louti)*

Family SERRANIDAE
Common Name White-lined rock-cod
Scientific Name *Anyperodon leucogrammicus* (Valenciennes), 1828
Habitat Coral reef
Distribution Qld., NT, WA
Depth Range 5 to 25 metres
Adult Size 50 centimetres
Food Habit Carnivorous: fish
Use Edible
Occurrence Moderately common

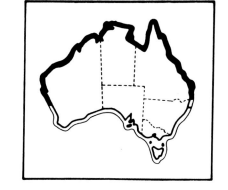

There have not been any large concentrations of white-lined rock-cods in the areas where I have dived on the Great Barrier Reef; one or two may be seen on a day's diving and most are juveniles. They inhabit open ledges, but are more likely to be seen around the edges of bommies and in reef gutters and chasms. Invariably, white-lined rock-cods swim with their head elevated and most can be easily approached. The juveniles have three to five opaque white lines running the length of the body and are a much lighter greenish yellow than the adults, which have very faint lines. Caught on fish baits and speared, their flesh is delicious.

White-lined rock-cod *(A. leucogrammicus)*

Family SERRANIDAE
Common Name Red-flushed rock-cod
Scientific Name *Aethaloperca rogaa* (Forsskål), 1775
Habitat Coral reef
Distribution Qld.
Depth Range 10 to 40 metres
Adult Size 60 centimetres
Food Habit Carnivorous: fish
Use Edible
Occurrence Uncommon

A. rogaa is a very characteristic fish having an all over black colour trimmed with a tinge of white on the edge of the caudal, anal and pelvic fins. An interesting feature is the bright orange colour, inside the mouth. The red-flushed rock-cod is not a very well known fish in Australia though it is caught quite regularly in some northern areas. It lives in caves and gutters in the reef and is difficult to find and photograph.

Red-flushed rock-cod *(A. rogaa)*

Family SERRANIDAE
Common Name Six-banded rock-cod
Scientific Name *Cephalopholis sexmaculatus* Ruppell, 1828
Habitat Coral reef, rocky reef
Distribution Qld. (also NSW)
Depth Range 20 to 40 metres
Adult Size 50 centimetres
Food Habit Carnivorous: fish, crustaceans
Use Edible
Occurrence Uncommon

Closely related to the coral rock-cod *C. miniatus*, *C. sexmaculatus* can be easily distinguished by its six dark perpendicular bands and the blue stripes in front of the eyes.

Only recently recorded from Australia, this species lives on offshore reefs and islands, the outer Great Barrier Reef and Coral Sea. It is not regularly caught and during the day it is quite secretive, living in deep caves and fissures in the reef, often in an upside down position.

C. sexmaculatus is a very shy species and will not allow close observation by divers.

Six-banded rock-cod *(C. sexmaculatus)*

Family SERRANIDAE
Common Name Coral rock-cod
Scientific Name *Cephalopholis miniatus* (Forsskål), 1775
Habitat Coral reef, rocky reef
Distribution Qld., NT, WA (also NSW)
Depth Range 10 to 40 metres
Adult Size 45 centimetres
Food Habit Carnivorous: fish, crustaceans
Use Edible
Occurrence Common

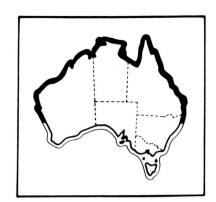

Sometimes mistaken for one of the coral trouts, *C. miniatus* can be distinguished by its larger blue spots, blue-edged fins, brighter red colour, deeper body, nine dorsal spines, and the rounded margin of the tail. A recent fauna survey at Lord Howe Island by AMPI explorers has recorded this fish at that location for the first time.

The coral cod is common in some areas, although it doesn't come out into the open as much as coral trout, preferring to stay in the confines of caves, ledges and coral labyrinths. This fish is caught on inshore and offshore reefs with fish bait, fights well when hooked and is as tasty as any coral trout, sometimes better.

Coral rock-cod *(C. miniatus)*

Family SERRANIDAE
Common Name Flag-tailed rock-cod
Scientific Name *Cephalopholis urodelus* (Valenciennes), 1828
Habitat Coral reef
Distribution Qld., WA
Depth Range 5 to 20 metres
Adult Size 23 centimetres
Food Habit Carnivorous: fish, crustaceans
Use Edible
Occurrence Common

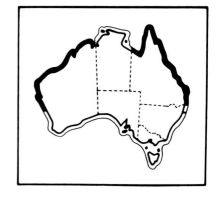

The flag-tailed rock-cod is a very conspicuous, little rock-cod, that may be black or red, with greenish patches of spots on the body. The lower lip is banded with black and light green and the leading edges of the dorsal and ventral fins are bright red. This little rock-cod is easily identified by the presence of two white lines on the tail, as depicted by the photograph. The tail is further bordered with bright red edges and there is a black spot at the top rear end of the gill cover.

C. urodelus is a diurnal species which sits out in the open supported by its pectoral fins and in this situation is fairly conspicuous. This species can be caught by line and although of small size is excellent eating.

Flag-tailed rock-cod *(C. urodelus)*

Family SERRANIDAE
Common Name Brown-banded rock-cod
Scientific Name *Cephalopholis pachycentron* (Valenciennes), 1828
Habitat Coral reef, rocky reef
Distribution Qld., NT, WA
Depth Range 5 to 20 metres
Adult Size 25 centimetres
Food Habit Carnivorous: crustaceans, fish
Use Edible
Occurrence Uncommon

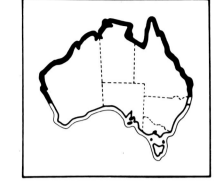

In many ways, the behaviour of the brown-banded rock-cod is similar to that of *E. homosinensis,* for it too lives under shallow ledges and holes in the coral and reef and is generally not seen out in the open during the day. *C. pachycentron* is not common and when observed, seems to prefer a head high position, propped up by its pectoral fins. Its colour varies from light brown to greenish brown with eight vertical bars of dark brown and some horizontal ones on the head. These bars are apt to fade on death. There is a distinct black blotch between the top two spines of the gill cover.

Brown-banded rock-cod *(C. pachycentron)*

Family SERRANDAE
Common Name Blue-spotted rock-cod
Scientific Name *Cephalopholis cyanostigma* (Valenciennes), 1828
Habitat Coral reef, rocky reef
Distribution Qld., NT (also NSW)
Depth Range 5 to 25 metres
Adult Size 35 centimetres
Food Habit Carnivorous: crustaceans, fish
Use Edible
Occurrence Common

C. cyanostigma, a resident of offshore islands and cays of the Great Barrier Reef is another attractive blue-spotted rock-cod. It is often seen behind a screen of staghorn coral in the shallows where it lies in wait for prey; in deeper water it sits out in the open amongst broken coral rubble and scattered coral clumps; in rocky reef areas it inhabits caves and ledges.

Distinguishing features are six obscure vertical bars (these are not always discernible on living fish) which are broken up by a patchwork of paler markings. Bright blue spots surrounded by darker ocelli cover the body, head and fins, and the tips of the spines on the dorsal fin are red. On living specimens there is also a very black patch at the rear top of the gill cover.

Blue-spotted rock-cod *(C. cyanostigma)*

Family SERRANIDAE
Common Name Barramundi rock-cod
Scientific Name *Cromileptes altivelis* (Valenciennes), 1828
Habitat Coral reef, rocky reef
Distribution Qld., NT, WA
Depth Range 5 to 20 metres
Adult Size 66 centimetres
Food Habit Carnivorous: fish
Use Edible
Occurrence Common

My first experience with a barramundi rock-cod was off Cairns, Queensland, in 1964, when an American spearfisherman brought in this strange looking fish to Upolo Cay. My second was in the Dampier Archipelago some seven years later, whilst on a fauna survey with the Western Australian Museum. I was just focusing in for my first picture when out of nowhere a spear transfixed it through the head, right in front of my camera. I finally got pictures of this interesting fish at Heron Island in 1974. Barramundi rock-cods were once a common species on most northern reefs but fishing pressure and their negligible fear of divers have reduced their numbers significantly. It's a pity that commercial fishes such as this are not more adequately known, or managed in some way.

Barramundi rock-cod *(C. altivelis)*

Family SERRANIDAE
Common Name Common coral trout
Scientific Name *Plectropoma leopardus* (Lacépède), 1802
Habitat Coral reefs
Distribution Qld.
Depth Range 3 to 50 metres
Adult Size 70 centimetres
Food Habit Carnivorous: fish, crustaceans
Use Edible
Occurrence Common

This species is the 'real' coral trout which is fished commercially through-out the Great Barrier Reef and which provides the excellent repasts on the tables and fish fries of many resorts.

The common coral trout is a relatively shallow water species and its most preferred depth during daylight hours seems to be between 5 and 10 metres. *P. leopardus* can be red, brown or dark grey and is covered all over with small blue dots. This fish is easily approached underwater and is very commonly speared. At night it sleeps beneath ledges and overhangs where it takes on a dappled shade of brown and pink. The common coral trout is handlined on cut fish, whole fish and is also taken on lures by trolling.

Common coral trout *(P. leopardus)*

Family SERRANIDAE
Common Name Footballer coral trout
Scientific Name *Plectropoma melanoleucus* Lacepede, 1802
Habitat Coral reef
Distribution Qld.
Depth Range 1 to 35 metres
Adult Size 63 centimetres
Food Habit Carnivorous: fish
Use Edible
Occurrence Uncommon

A bit of an enigma for quite some time, the footballer coral trout was in the past thought to be only a colour variation, or phase of *P. maculatus,* although it is now recognised as a quite separate species.

The footballer coral trout has unique colours and patterns and once seen is never forgotten. It lives around offshore coral reefs in certain areas and is by no means commonly encountered.

Unlike other coral trouts, *P. melanoleucus* is a very shy fish which moves down the reef slopes into deeper water when approached by divers. Examples have been boated off the central Great Barrier Reef and as far south as the Capricorn group. They are good eating.

Footballer coral trout *(P. melanoleucus)*

Family SERRANIDAE
Common Name Oceanic coral trout
Scientific Name *Plectropoma* sp.
Habitat Coral reef
Distribution Qld.
Depth Range 20 to 50 metres
Adult Size 1.5 metres
Food Habit Carnivorous: fish, crustaceans
Use Edible
Occurrence Uncommon

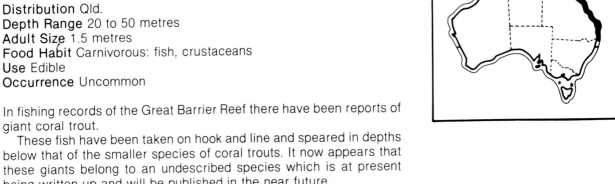

In fishing records of the Great Barrier Reef there have been reports of giant coral trout.

These fish have been taken on hook and line and speared in depths below that of the smaller species of coral trouts. It now appears that these giants belong to an undescribed species which is at present being written up and will be published in the near future.

The oceanic coral trout is only found on the outer islands and cays of the Great Barrier Reef. This species has a characteristic colour pattern which appears to be quite constant. The oceanic coral trout is good eating and can weigh up to 20 kg; it is very wary.

Oceanic coral trout (*Plectropoma* sp.)

Family SERRANIDAE
Common Name Island coral trout
Scientific Name *Plectropoma maculatus* (Bloch), 1790
Habitat Rocky reef, coral reef
Distribution Qld., NT, WA
Depth Range 1 to 60 metres
Adult Size 60 centimetres
Food Habit Carnivorous: fish
Use Edible
Occurrence Common

Due to recent studies undertaken by the Queensland Fisheries Service, it is now known that there are at least five species of coral trouts inhabiting the reefs of northern Australia, where previously only one or two were thought to exist.

The island coral trout occurs on inshore reefs and continental islands, from Yeppoon Queensland, around to Shark Bay in Western Australia. *P. maculatus* is reddish brown in colour, though it can also be various shades of brown or grey, as well. Its main distinguishing features are the elongated bright blue dashes on the head, cheeks and gill cover. This fish is easily approached underwater and is easily caught on most fish baits during the day. Like all coral trout it is an excellent food fish.

Island coral trout *(P. maculatus)*

Family SERRANIDAE
Common Name Potato rock-cod
Scientific Name *Epinephelus tukula* Morgans, 1959
Habitat Coral reef, rocky reef
Distribution Qld., WA
Depth Range 10 to 40 metres
Adult Size 1.5 metres
Food Habit Carnivorous: fish, crustaceans
Use Edible
Occurrence Uncommon

The first knowledge of this fish in Australian waters was from a photograph I took off north Western Australia in 1971, yet it wasn't until 1975 when I again photographed it off Yonga Reef on the northern Great Barrier Reef that identification was verified. The potato rock-cod is a large predator that is generally seen on offshore reefs and islands, along the faces of drop offs and channel slopes where it inhabits grottoes and reef channels open to the sea. During the day it sometimes patrols along the sea floor but rarely is it very far away from the reef. Easily tamed underwater, this fish is now protected in certain areas of the Great Barrier Reef and north Western Australia. They are taken by handline on occasion and speared. Smaller specimens make fine eating.

Potato rock-cod *(E. tukula)*

Family SERRANIDAE
Common Name Long-finned rock-cod
Scientific Name *Epinephelus megachir* (Richardson), 1846
Habitat Coral reef, rocky reef
Distribution Qld., NT, WA
Depth Range 3 to 20 metres
Adult Size 45 centimetres
Food Habit Carnivorous: fish, crustaceans
Use Edible
Occurrence Common

A small easily recognised, diurnal predator, *E. megachir* occurs on mainland reefs, continental islands and offshore coral islands and cays.

It has a very large hexagonal pattern when compared to other wire-netting rock-cods and its pectoral fins are plain and much longer, with only a light coloured bar at the base and a few scattered yellow speckles. In shallow water it may be found hiding beneath the edges of fallen staghorn coral plates; in deeper water it sits out in the open propped up on its ventrals in a 'wait and watch' attitude. It will devour anything resembling fish, and also eats crabs. Despite its small size it has white, firm, moist flesh.

Long-finned rock-cod *(E. megachir)*

Family SERRANIDAE
Common Name Wavy-lined rock-cod
Scientific Name *Epinephelus summana* (Forsskål), 1775
Habitat Coral reef, rocky reef, mangroves
Distribution Qld.
Depth Range 5 to 25 metres
Adult Size 50 centimetres
Food Habit Carnivorous: fish, crustaceans
Use Edible
Occurrence Common

Unlike a lot of rock-cods, this one seems to be as prevalent on the coast as it is on continental islands and offshore reefs. In quite a number of locations it may be caught on lines and in nets in mainland estuaries, occasionally venturing into freshwater.

The wavy-lined rock-cod has a very distinctive pattern. On the Great Barrier Reef it can be seen under high ledges and caves and seems to prefer sandy patches. It will accept fish bait quite readily and although small, should not be discarded, as it makes quite a good food fish.

Wavy-lined rock-cod *(E. summana)*

Family SERRANIDAE
Common Name Black-tipped rock-cod
Scientific Name *Epinephelus fasciatus* (Forsskål), 1775
Habitat Coral reef, rocky reef
Distribution Qld., NT, WA (also NSW)
Depth Range 5 to 60 metres
Adult Size 38 centimetres
Food Habit Carnivorous: fish, crustaceans
Use Edible
Occurrence Common

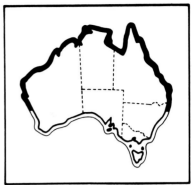

Perched on some high projection on the reef, *E. fasciatus* is always ready to launch itself at some unwary passerby. It is a behavioural trait of this fish to choose elevated hunting platforms and this habit is the same in shallow or deep water. The black-tipped rock-cod can be caught, or seen, on the mainland reefs, continental and offshore coral islands and cays. Shallow water fish are white to pink in colour with light brown perpendicular bands, whereas deeper water fish are bright red or orange, with six to seven darker bands. Wherever the fish is seen it can always be readily identified by the intense black edging to its dorsal fin, with each dorsal spine ending in a white tip. This little fish is very good to eat.

Black-tipped rock-cod *(E. fasciatus)*

Family SERRANIDAE
Common Name Giant groper
Scientific Name *Epinephelus lanceolatus* (Bloch), 1790
Habitat Coral reef, rocky reef
Distribution Qld., NT, WA
Depth Range 10 to 50 metres
Adult Size 3 metres
Food Habit Carnivorous: fish, crustaceans
Use Edible
Occurrence Common

In the heyday of Australian spearfishing these giant fish were methodically massacred for pointscore records and, often, simply because they were there. Frequently the carcasses were left to rot on the beaches, or were dumped in the shallows to wash up as bloated monuments to man's irresponsibility. Today's divers are much more environmentally conscious and see the need for the conservation of such large fish. Although giant groper are credited with attacks on pearl divers there are no authentic records of fatalities.

This fish rivals the greasy rock-cod, *E. tauvina*, in size and colouration; they can be separated as *E. tauvina* has an angular preoperculum and *E. lanceolatus* has a rounded preoperculum. Giant gropers are edible as juveniles but are coarse and tasteless when large.

Giant groper *(E. lanceolatus)*

Family SERRANIDAE
Common Name Brown-spotted rock-cod, greasy rock-cod
Scientific Name *Epinephelus tauvina* (Forsskål), 1775
Habitat Coral reef, rocky reef, jetty piles, mangroves
Distribution Qld., NT, WA (also NSW)
Depth Range 1 to 50 metres
Adult Size 2.5 metres
Food Habit Carnivorous: fish, crustaceans, reptiles
Use Edible
Occurrence Common

Meeting any large fish is apt to be a little disconcerting underwater, sometimes more so than others. The brown-spotted rock-cod grows quite large and in the often murky waters of the North Coast mainland, such a fish met head on, can boost your adrenalin output dramatically.

These excellent eating fish (up to 50 kg) are fairly common inhabitants of mainland and offshore areas throughout their range and despite their size have not been proved to attack man. They are easily approached underwater and, as well as being speared in large numbers, they are caught by line and, surprisingly enough, by lures. Their normal food is comprised of fish and crabs, which they swallow whole.

Brown-spotted rock-cod *(E. tauvina)*

Family SERRANIDAE
Common Name Flowery rock-cod
Scientific Name *Epinephelus fuscoguttatus* (Forsskål), 1775
Habitat Coral reef, rocky reef, mangroves
Distribution Qld., NT, WA (also NSW)
Depth Range 1 to 25 metres
Adult Size 1 metre
Food Habit Carnivorous: fish, crustaceans
Use Edible
Occurrence Common

In the past decade, Australia has come a long way towards the recognition and identification of fishes in their own environment. It wasn't so many years ago that the standard answer from institutions of science to photographers was, go get the fish. Much of this knowledge has been brought about by the efforts of underwater photographers, naturalists, and more recently, underwater ichthyologists. The flowery rock-cod when first photographed twelve years ago, remained unidentified for several years afterwards, though it is well known today. This fish lives on mainland and offshore reefs throughout northern Australia, generally inhabiting caves, or overhanging ledges. It bites well on fish bait, is easily approached underwater and is an excellent food fish.

Flowery rock-cod *(E. fuscoguttatus)*

Family SERRANIDAE
Common Name Chinaman rock-cod
Scientific Name *Epinephelus homosinensis* Whitley, 1944
Habitat Rocky reef, coral reef
Distribution WA
Depth Range 1 to 100 metres
Adult Size 25 centimetres
Food Habit Carnivorous: fish, crustaceans
Use Edible
Occurrence Uncommon

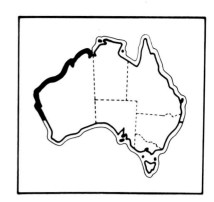

Endemic to Western Australia, the Chinaman rock-cod ranges from Fremantle, north to North West Cape. Throughout its range this little rock-cod is not particularly common, though places like Houtman Abrolhos off Geraldton, are an exception. It inhabits both inshore and offshore reefs and may be taken in moderately deep water.

These fish are numerous in shallow water and despite their shyness can be encouraged out into the open, for similar to many carnivores they are very inquisitive. Although caught by line, many are thrown back due to their small size. The colours of the fish range from rusty red to green, the five dark brown bands on the body are fairly stable features.

Chinaman rock-cod *(E. homosinensis)*

Family SERRANIDAE
Common Name Bird-wire rock-cod
Scientific Name *Epinephelus chlorostigma* (Valenciennes), 1828
Habitat Rocky reef, coral reef
Distribution WA
Depth Range 5 to 25 metres
Adult Size 63 centimetres
Food Habit Carnivorous: fish, molluscs, crustaceans
Use Edible
Occurrence Moderately common

There are four similarly patterned rock-cods inhabiting the reefs of Northern Australia and there has been a good deal of confusion regarding their identification.

The bird-wire rock-cod is only found in north Western Australia and of the wire-netting rock-cod complex, this one grows the largest. Bird-wire rock-cods are found in vast limestone caverns and under ledges at mainland and offshore islands and appear to be much shyer than their eastern relatives. They can be hooked on fish bait, though some are lost due to their habit of grabbing the bait and heading for a hole, or the coral. The tail on this species has a straight edge.

Bird-wire rock-cod *(E. chlorostigma)*

Family SERRANIDAE
Common Name Wire-netting rock cod
Scientific Name *Epinephelus merra* Bloch, 1793
Habitat Coral reef, rocky reef
Distribution Qld., NT, WA (also NSW)
Depth Range Intertidal to 25 metres
Adult Size 45 centimetres
Food Habit Carnivorous: fish, crustaceans
Use Edible
Occurrence Common

A very common resident of mainland and offshore areas in the vicinity of coral reefs, or muddy rocky reefs, the wire-netting rock-cod is one of the smaller rock-cods which, although regularly caught by line, hardly warrants a second glance from an enterprising spearfisherman. I must admit I am not too proud to eat a few wire-nettings, as they have a beautiful flavour and firm, moist, white flesh.

The wire-netting rock-cod is often confused with the long-finned rock-cod, sometimes even by those who should know better. A simple method of distinguishing between them is to look closely at the pectoral fin. On *E. merra* the pectoral is entirely covered with small brown spots. On *E. megachir* the pectoral is longer and has only a few indistinct white, or yellow specks.

Wire-netting rock-cod *(E. merra)*

Family SERRANIDAE
Common Name Purple rock-cod
Scientific Name *Epinephelus flavocaeruleus* (Lacépède), 1802
Habitat Coral reef, rocky reef
Distribution Qld.
Depth Range 10 to 30 metres
Adult Size 1 metre
Food Habit Carnivorous: fish
Use Edible
Occurrence Uncommon

Found throughout the Great Barrier Reef, the purple rock-cod tends to be a bluish grey in life with a peppered coating of black dots. It presents no problems in identification for its colours and patterns are unlike any other rock-cod.

Very few of this species are seen underwater and where they occur around offshore reefs they tend to swim in the water column above the reef during the day, patrolling backwards and forwards. At night they move out to deeper water.

Due to their swimming several metres above the bottom they are not always easily approached and at times appear shy. They can be caught by line on fish bait and make excellent eating, having firm, white flesh.

Purple rock-cod *(E. flavocaeruleus)*

Family SERRANIDAE
Common Name Trout rock-cod
Scientific Name *Epinephelus fario* (Thunberg), 1793
Habitat Coral reef, rocky reef
Distribution Qld., WA
Depth Range 8 to 25 metres
Adult Size 45 centimetres
Food Habit Carnivorous: fish, crustaceans
Use Edible
Occurrence Uncommon

The trout rock-cod was first recorded from Queensland. When I photographed it in north Western Australia in 1971 it was unrecorded from that state.

   E. fario has a very elongated head and is fairly simple to identify. Its colour ranges from off-white to deep green, with light blotches covered with dark brown to black, widely separated equidistant spots. This fish resides in caves and beneath ledges during the day and is rarely caught by handline, or spear.

Trout rock-cod *(E. fario)*

Family SERRANIDAE
Common Name Orange fairy basslet
Scientific Name *Anthias squammipinnis* (Peters), 1855
Habitat Coral reef, rocky reef
Distribution Qld. (also NSW)
Depth Range 10 to 40 metres
Adult Size 11 centimetres
Food Habit Carnivorous: zooplankton
Use Aquarium fish
Occurrence Common

I think fairy basslets are the jewels of the sea and whenever one dives in the tropics these little fish, of one species or another, are almost always present. Orange fairy basslets are the most common and widespread of all the Australian fairy basslets and as well as being found throughout the entire Great Barrier Reef, also occur in New South Wales as far south as Ulladulla. Orange fairy basslets are seen on the tops of dropoffs, bommies and reef edges and are especially prolific on coral heads behind the Great Barrier Reef proper. As there can be up to 30 or 40 females all feeding I am not sure how the few males, who are constantly darting at each other, maintain a territorial space; perhaps they just chase other males away from the females.

Orange fairy basslet *(A. squammipinnis)*, female. Inset: male

Family SERRANIDAE
Common Name Purple queenfish
Scientific Name *Anthias tuka* (Herre and Montalban), 1927
Habitat Coral reef
Distribution Qld. (also NSW)
Depth Range 10 to 30 metres
Adult Size 12 centimetres
Food Habit Carnivorous: zooplankton
Use Aquarium fish
Occurrence Uncommon

To say that this little fish is spectacular is an understatement, and even though the photographs adequately portray them, there is nothing that compares with being poised on top of a coral head, over a 30 metre drop-off in crystal clear water and virtually surrounded by dozens of purple queens. These gems of nature generally swim in small, or large groups consisting mostly of females. Colour varies from blue to purple and sometimes pink. Males spend a lot of their time chasing other males away from their territory. The common name refers to the male.

Purple queenfish *(A. tuka)*, female. Inset: male

Family SERRANIDAE
Common Name Blotched fairy basslet
Scientific Name *Anthias pleurotaenia* Bleeker, 1857
Habitat Coral reef
Distribution Qld.
Depth Range 10 to 30 metres
Adult Size 11 centimetres
Food Habit Carnivorous: zooplankton
Use Aquarium fish
Occurrence Uncommon

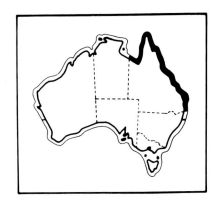

An absolutely exquisite, highly coloured and easily identified species, *A. pleurotaenia* must capture the imagination of every fish enthusiast. Sadly, only divers are able to enjoy the blotched fairy basslet as it lives in the clear waters off the northern Great Barrier Reef and Coral Sea. Blotched fairy basslet may be seen feeding in the water column several metres above the bottom, close to cliff faces, or on the slopes of underwater reefs.

During the breeding season males are territorial and set up special areas such as a specific gorgonian sea fan, or a ledge of dead reef. In areas where these fish abound there may be a male every few metres. They seem to all congregate in one specific place and compete for the females.

Blotched fairy basslet *(A. pleurotaenia)*, male. Inset: female

Family SERRANIDAE
Common Name Hucht's fairy basslet
Scientific Name *Anthias huchtii* Bleeker, 1857
Habitat Coral reef
Distribution Qld.
Depth Range 5 to 10 metres
Adult Size 11 centimetres
Food Habit Carnivorous: zooplankton
Use Aquarium fish
Occurrence Moderately common

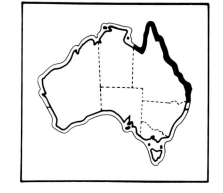

An easily-recognised species, this fish was only recently recorded from Australia. *A. huchtii* is a shallow water anthiad which occurs on the tops of reefs and bommies along the northern outer areas of the Great Barrier Reef. Not as common as some other species of fairy basslets, it generally has a ratio of six to eight females to one male.

These fishes are planktivores and spend a lot of their time in the water column above the reef, feeding on small micro-organisms drifting past.

Hucht's fairy basslet *(A. huchtii)*, male. Inset: female

Family PSEUDOCHROMIDAE
Common Name Bicolor cichlops
Scientific Name *Pseudochromis paccagnellae* Axelrod, 1973
Habitat Coral reef
Distribution Qld.
Depth Range 10 to 35 metres
Adult Size 7 centimetres
Food Habit Carnivorous: crustaceans
Use Aquarium fish
Occurrence Uncommon

A shy and rather timid species, the bicolor cichlops is often seen in fissures in bommies and in areas where one coral head is undercut and flanked by another. They are territorial and patrol along several metres of vertical reef face searching for food. They are more numerous in deeper water of 15 to 35 metres and swim in a head high position.

This species is a favourite with marine aquarists and is fairly easily maintained in an aquarium. It is captured in increasing numbers for the trade in many parts of the Indo-Pacific region, where it is much more widespread than formerly believed.

Bicolor cichlops *(P. paccagnellae)*

Family PLESIOPIDAE
Common Name Macneill's assessor
Scientific Name *Assessor macneilli* Whitley, 1935
Habitat Coral reef
Distribution Qld.
Depth Range 5 to 20 metres
Adult Size 4 centimetres
Food Habit Carnivorous: crustaceans
Use Aquarium fish
Occurrence Common

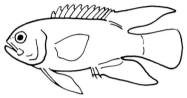

Macneill's assessor is a very common and easily overlooked species which lives on offshore reefs and cays along the entire Great Barrier Reef. The reason it is rarely noticed by divers is due to its dark blue colour and the fact that it inhabits crevices and ledges, where it swims upside down, often in a vertical position.

To photograph these elusive little fish requires lots of patience and determination for they are rarely still and swim in a manner which makes focusing difficult. Rudie Kuiter of Melbourne has discovered that *A. macneilli* spawns in summer and that the male incubates the eggs in its mouth; incubation takes 15 to 16 days, during which time the male does not feed.

Macneill's assessor *(A. macneilli)*

Family PLESIOPIDAE
Common Name Yellow assessor
Scientific Name *Assessor flavissimus* Allen and Kuiter, 1976
Habitat Coral reef
Distribution Qld.
Depth Range 5 to 20 metres
Adult Size 4 centimetres
Food Habit Carnivorous: crustaceans
Use Aquarium fish
Occurrence Common

Whereas Macneill's assessor is found along the entire length of the Great Barrier Reef *A. flavissimus* has only been recorded from reefs off Cairns, Queensland, northward. The yellow assessor is found in the same type of territory as Macneill's assessor, preferring low caves and ledges with sandy bottoms. In many cases both species can be seen in the same cave, while at other locations they may be separate.

The most *A. flavissimus* I have ever seen in one cave numbered around 18 specimens; it is very difficult to get an accurate estimate due to the fishes' continuous swimming in and out of the light.

Yellow assessor *(A. flavissimus)*

Family PRIACANTHIDAE
Common Name Lunar-tailed glasseye
Scientific Name *Priacanthus hamrur* (Forsskål), 1775
Habitat Coral reef
Distribution Qld., NT
Depth Range 5 to 25 metres
Adult Size 40 centimetres
Food Habit Carnivorous: free-swimming crustaceans, cephalopods
Use Edible
Occurrence Common

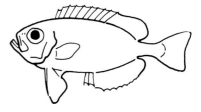

Found throughout the entire Great Barrier Reef system, *P. hamrur* is generally a nocturnal species which is often observed during night diving excursions, at which time it can be found over reefs, or sometimes over sand and rubble. As with many fish, the day colour pattern differs from the night colouration of pinkish mottled spots. During the day it shelters beneath ledges, or behind coral cover and is rarely seen out in the open. Towards late afternoon some individuals may emerge but these tend to keep very close to the protection of the coral.

Lunar-tailed glasseyes have black fins and can be caught on handlines.

Lunar-tailed glasseye *(P. hamrur)*

Family APOGONIDAE
Common Name Red-barred cardinalfish
Scientific Name *Archamia fucata* (Cantor), 1850
Habitat Coral reef, rocky reef
Distribution Qld.
Depth Range 4 to 20 metres
Adult Size 7 centimetres
Food Habit Carnivorous: crustaceans
Use Aquarium fish
Occurrence Common

A beautifully marked species, *A. fucata* inhabits the Northern Great Barrier Reef where it is found in colonies living amongst corals under sheltered conditions. During the day it hovers in the complex of fissures and branched coral havens. Occasionally solitary, or paired specimens, may reside in caves.

   At dusk the fish commences to move from the depths of the coral clumps to the outer periphery, retreating into the coral at the slightest hint of danger. At night they can be found in the open, above the coral, or on the bottom, feeding on small crustaceans.

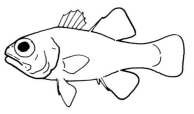

Red-barred cardinalfish *(A. fucata)*

Family APOGONIDAE
Common Name Five-lined cardinalfish
Scientific Name *Cheilodipterus quinquelineata* (Cuvier), 1828
Habitat Coral reef, rocky reef
Distribution Qld., NT, WA (also NSW)
Depth Range 2 to 20 metres
Adult Size 10 centimetres
Food Habit Carnivorous: crustaceans
Use Aquarium fish
Occurrence Common

To the novice, cardinalfishes with stripes all tend to look identical, though they are fairly simple to identify with a good colour reference.

Each one has a feature by which it can be recognised. The five-lined cardinalfish as its name implies has five lines running from the snout to the base of the tail where there is a black spot surrounded by a bright yellow patch, on the caudal peduncle.

Five-lined cardinalfishes are seen during the day sheltering beneath ledges, and in caves with sand bottoms. They feed at night and are generally observed alone.

Five-lined cardinalfish *(C. quinquelineata)*

Family APOGONIDAE
Common Name Big-toothed cardinalfish
Scientific Name *Cheilodipterus macrodon* (Lacepede), 1802
Habitat Coral reef, rocky reef
Distribution Qld., NT, WA, (also NSW)
Depth Range 8 to 25 metres
Adult Size 20 centimetres
Food Habit Carnivorous: crustaceans
Use Aquarium fish
Occurrence Common

One of the largest cardinalfishes, this species inhabits both inshore and offshore reefs, and during the day can be seen beneath ledges, in caves, and on the floor of deeper reef fissures, in subdued light.

My photographs taken off north Western Australia in 1971 were the first record of this species in that state.

C. macrodon is a solitary species and in many areas it is relatively shy, always facing headfirst into a ledge or crevice whenever it is approached too closely. However, during the breeding season pairs may be observed, at which time the male may be seen to have an enlarged mouth and throat due to the incubating eggs in its mouth.

Big-toothed cardinalfish *(C. macrodon)*

Family APOGONIDAE
Common Name Blue-striped cardinalfish
Scientific Name *Apogon cyanosoma* Bleeker, 1853
Habitat Coral reef, rocky reef
Distribution Qld., WA
Depth Range 10 to 20 metres
Adult Size 10 centimetres
Food Habit Carnivorous: crustaceans
Use Aquarium fish
Occurrence Uncommon

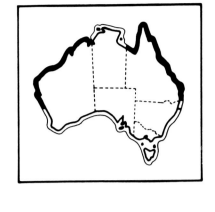

One of the more recently recorded *Apogon* species in Australia, *A. cyanosoma* comes from the continental islands and the reefs and cays of the northern section of the Great Barrier Reef. It may be solitary, or in pairs, beneath ledges and caves, and is not difficult to approach.

This species is an excellent example of the difference beteween dead fishes and live ones. In life *A. cyanosoma* has blue stripes on a brilliant gold background. When it is dead the colours reverse and the fish has brilliant gold stripes on a palid silvery blue-grey background. What is even more interesting is the fact that this happens with the same stripes, not adjacent ones.

Changes of this nature cause a great deal of confusion as most scienticfic descriptions relate to dead fishes. Consequently the early underwater photographs of living fishes were not easily identified by ichthyologists, who demanded the specimen as well.

Blue-striped cardinalfish *(A. cyanosoma)*

Family APOGONIDAE
Common Name Doederlein's cardinalfish
Scientific Name *Apogon doederleini* Jordan and Snyder, 1901
Habitat Coral reef, rocky reef
Distribution Qld., WA (also NSW)
Depth Range 3 to 10 metres
Adult Size 12 centimetres
Food Habit Carnivorous: crustaceans
Use Aquarium fish
Occurrence Common

Widely distributed throughout the entire Great Barrier Reef and the Coral Sea, *A. doederleini* lives beneath shallow ledges that have a sandy floor. This species is mostly solitary and is easily approached. *A. doederleini* is a nocturnal forager feeding on small shrimps and other crustaceans.

Most adults have a pink colouration, though semi-adults may be silver. The four black lines which run from the front of the fish down to the back are characteristic, although they vary in width sometimes. There is a black spot without a halo, on the tail.

Doederlein's cardinalfish *(A. doederleini)*

Family APOGONIDAE
Common Name Kallopterus cardinalfish
Scientific Name *Apogon kallopterus* Bleeker, 1856
Habitat Coral reef
Distribution Qld.
Depth Range 8 to 20 metres
Adult Size 10 centimetres
Food Habit Carnivorous: crustaceans
Use Aquarium fish
Occurrence Moderately common

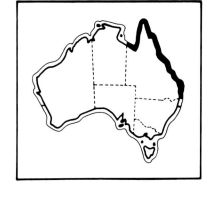

This species can be found around bommies and coral heads in lagoons, and the lee sides of islands and cays of the northern Great Barrier Reef. Generally a solitary fish, it can be recognised by its very coarse scale pattern, yellow dorsal fin, and the wide black stripe which runs from the snout through the eye and down to the tail. There is a large black spot on the caudal peduncle.

   Due to the time of day and the fishes' mood, the heavy body stripes may be reduced in length and width towards the tail.

Kallopterus cardinalfish *(A. kallopterus)*

Family CARANGIDAE
Common Name Rainbow runner
Scientific Name *Elagatis bipinnulatus* (Quoy and Gaimard), 1824
Habitat Open ocean, coral reef, rocky reef
Distribution Qld., NT, WA (also NSW)
Depth Range Surface to 50 metres
Adult Size 1.2 metres
Food Habit Carnivorous: fish
Use Edible
Occurrence Common

Generally caught in the vicinity of coral reefs, rocky reefs, and in open ocean around the peaks of sea mounts, the rainbow runner inhabits both inshore and offshore areas.

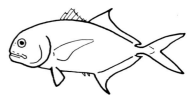

Similar to other carangids *(Seriola)* schools of these fishes often follow larger fishes around (and vice-versa), and will at times herald the presence of sharks, giant stingrays and tuna. Their shoaling behaviour is not one of a tight formation; most individuals seem to maintain a wider spatial zoning than other carangids. When in the vicinity of offshore reefs, individuals often leave the school and swim to a cleaner-fish station. They are very nervy and erratic when being cleaned.

Rainbow runners bite hard and fight well on light gear. They are frequently taken when trolling for Spanish mackerel.

Rainbow runner *(E. bipinnulatus)*

Family CARANGIDAE
Common Name Embury's turrum
Scientific Name *Carangoides emburyi* (Whitley), 1932
Habitat Coral reef, sand, rubble
Distribution Qld., NT
Depth Range Surface to 40 metres
Adult Size 1.3 metres
Food Habit Carnivorous: fish, crustaceans
Use Edible
Occurrence Common

Widely distributed along the Great Barrier Reef and adjacent mainland, *C. emburyi* swims in fairly large schools. It feeds on sandy or sandy rubble bottom where it sorts out the molluscs, worms and crustaceans from mouthfuls of sand which are ejected via the gill covers. When hooked they are extremely strong fighters and by the time you have landed a 22 kilogram turrum, you've earned him. Large turrum will bite on cut fish baits and also rise to lures. The larger specimens may have somewhat coarse flesh but they are still pretty good eating.

Embury's turrum *(C. emburyi)*

Family CARANGIDAE
Common Name Gold-spotted trevally
Scientific Name *Carangoides fulvoguttatus* (Forsskål), 1775
Habitat Coral reef
Distribution Qld., WA, NT
Depth Range 5 to 40 metres
Adult Size 1 metre
Food Habit Carnivorous: fish, crustaceans
Use Edible
Occurrence Common

The offshore waters of the Great Barrier Reef and the continental islands and reefs of north Western Australia are the favourite habitat of this fish. Closer to the mainland, juveniles may school, although adult *C. fulvoguttatus* are mostly observed in pairs or small groups of 4 or 5 fish. They are a fast swimming cautious species and rarely come back for a second look.

The gold-spotted trevally can be caught on cut fish bait in shallow lagoons and also by trolling around coral heads, or the edges of back reefs. They are an excellent fighting fish, and good to eat.

Gold-spotted trevally *(C. fulvoguttatus)*

Family CARANGIDAE
Common Name Golden trevally
Scientific Name *Gnathanodon speciosus* (Forsskål), 1775
Habitat Coral reef, rocky reef, sand, rubble
Distribution Qld., NT, WA (also NSW)
Depth Range 5 to 40 metres
Adult Size 1.2 metres
Food Habit Carnivorous: fish, molluscs, crustaceans
Use Edible
Occurrence Common

Commonly seen in schools, golden trevally also swim in pairs or small groups, especially when feeding on the bottom. When the fish are feeding their colour intensifies and resembles the deep gold of dead fish; normally they are silvery with yellowish head and fins and with darker cross bars. The minute teeth of the juvenile fish are entirely lost with age. Golden trevally can be caught on cut fish bait and are fairly good to eat. These fish occur on inshore and offshore reefs throughout this range.

Golden trevally *(G. speciosus)*

Family CARANGIDAE
Common Name Bigeye trevally
Scientific Name *Caranx sexfasciatus* Quoy and Gaimard, 1824
Habitat Coral reef, rocky reef
Distribution Qld., NT, WA (also NSW)
Depth Range 5 to 60 metres
Adult Size 1.4 metres
Food Habit Carnivorous: fish, crustaceans
Use Edible
Occurrence Common

Big, exciting fish, hundreds of them all around you in a huge school, fish in every direction, milling, swimming, banking, wall-to-wall fish, totally mindblowing and then nothing, just empty blue. You can't believe it happened, and then you remember your camera . . . Such is the experience of *C. sexfasciatus* underwater, and sometimes I am asked why I gave up fishing with a line?

Bigeye trevally are an inshore and offshore species common in more northern areas.

Occasionally fishermen confuse the bigeye trevally with turrum. *C. sexfasciatus* is a slimmer fish with 19 to 21 rays in the soft dorsal fin and a very distinctive black blotch on the top of the gill cover; the soft dorsal fin is black with a white tip.

Bigeye trevally (*C. sexfasciatus*)

Family CARANGIDAE
Common Name Giant trevally
Scientific Name *Caranx ignobilis* (Forsskål), 1775
Habitat Coral reef
Distribution Qld., NT, WA
Depth Range 1 to 30 metres
Adult Size 1.4 metres
Food Habit Carnivorous: fish, crustaceans
Use Edible
Occurrence Common

Large giant trevally often swim alone, or in pairs, and inhabit offshore reefs and cays. In many localities they are commonly caught by bottom fishing and at times by trolling with lures. *C. ignobilis* occur in shallow or deep water, either on the reef front, or behind. They also enter lagoons and when excited by bait are extremely pugnacious, even taking food from sharks. The fins are dark in colour, there is no black spot on the operculum, and the caudal peduncle scutes have a number of black bands; there is a white edge to the ventral fin.

Giant trevally *(C. ignobilis)*

Family CARANGIDAE
Common Name Blue-fin trevally
Scientific Name *Caranx melampygus* Cuvier, 1833
Habitat Coral reef, rocky reef
Distribution Qld., WA
Depth Range 5 to 40 metres
Adult Size 68 centimetres
Food Habit Carnivorous: fish, crustaceans
Use Edible
Occurrence Common

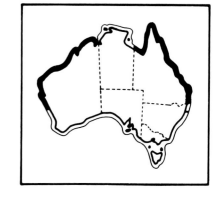

The blue-fin trevally occurs on mainland and continental island reefs, the Great Barrier and the Coral Sea.

Blue-fin trevallies usually swim in pairs, though a group of four to six is not uncommon. They inhabit both open reef fronts, as well as sheltered lagoons, and will approach a diver at close quarters to make one or two passes before going their way.

The second dorsal fin, the caudal and the anal fins are bright blue, with a scattering of darker blue or black spots over the head and upper half of the body in adults. It can be caught on fish bait, on the bottom and is sometimes caught by trolling lures.

Blue-fin trevally *(C. melampygus)*

Family CARANGIDAE
Common Name Amberjack
Scientific Name *Seriola dumerili* (Risso), 1810
Habitat Rocky reef, coral reef
Distribution Qld. (also NSW)
Depth Range 10 to 50 metres
Adult Size 1.5 metres
Food Habit Carnivorous: fish
Use Edible
Occurrence Uncommon

When you only have a black and white line-drawing to go on, and no living colour record or distinguishing visual feature, there are times when you wonder if you will ever recognise such species when you see them underwater. I dived some 16 years before I saw my first amberjack alive, yet I recognised it instantly.

S. *dumerili* is not as common as the yellowtail kingfish, to which it is closely related, (see *Australian Sea Fishes South of 30°S*) and it doesn't appear to school in large numbers. It can be caught by trolling on the surface and also on fish bait while bottom fishing.

Besides being mauve coloured on the back, S. *dumerili* has a yellow median stripe from the gill cover through to the tail and a black stripe from the nose, through the eye, to the dorsal fin.

Amberjack *(S. dumerili)*

Family LUTJANIDAE
Common Name Pedley's fusilier
Scientific Name *Paracaesio pedleyi* McCulloch and Waite, 1916
Habitat Coral reef, rocky reef
Distribution Qld., WA, NT
Depth Range 5 to 25 metres
Adult Size 35 centimetres
Food Habit Carnivorous: zooplankton
Use Edible
Occurrence Common

Generally found on the offshore areas of the Great Barrier Reef, on the east coast, *P. pedleyi* is quite commonly observed on the inshore and offshore reefs on the North-Western coast. This species swims in large schools along the faces of reef fronts, also in channels and the cliff edges of back reefs.

These vividly coloured fish are an incredible sight when they visit a cleaner-fish station; tailstanding and flashing their colours on and off, they turn darker blue when being cleaned.

Pedley's fusilier feed on zooplankton and will bite on prawn bait; it is a good table fish providing it is bled immediately on capture, but will not keep unless frozen quickly.

Pedley's fusilier *(P. pedleyi)*

Family LUTJANIDAE
Common Name Chinaman fish
Scientific Name *Symphorus nematophorus* (Bleeker), 1860
Habitat Coral reef, rocky reef
Distribution Qld., NT, WA
Depth Range 8 to 80 metres
Adult Size 1 metre
Food Habit Carnivorous: fish, crustaceans
Use Non-edible
Occurrence Common

A large snapper with a round forehead, this species is recognised by its colour and conspicuous groove before the eye. Over sand the background colour may change to pink with numerous blue lines running the length of the body. Younger fish have long filaments on the soft dorsal fin.

Chinaman fish are widespread on the Great Barrier Reef and are common in the northern areas, often seen in groups of four to six individuals. It will bite aggressively on fish bait and, although eaten in some areas, it has caused ciguatera, or fish poisoning, and for this reason is generally avoided.

Chinaman fish *(S. nematophorus)*

Family LUTJANIDAE
Common Name Four-lined snapper
Scientific Name *Lutjanus kasmira* (Forsskål), 1775
Habitat Coral reef, rocky reef
Distribution Qld., NT, WA (also NSW)
Depth Range 10 to 30 metres
Adult Size 38 centimetres
Food Habit Carnivorous: fish, crustaceans
Use Edible
Occurrence Common

Exquisitely coloured, this fish inhabits inshore reefs, continental islands, and the Great Barrier Reef. It is commonly seen in the open around coral heads where there are large caves and fissures. *L. kasmira* is sometimes difficult to approach underwater, and although they school, most swim in small groups, rarely alone. Throughout their wide distribution they do not appear in large numbers at any one location. This little snapper is very good eating and may be caught on a variety of fish or the shrimp baits during the day or night.

Four-lined snapper *(L. kasmira)*

Family LUTJANIDAE
Common Name Blacktail snapper
Scientific Name *Lutjanus fulvus* (Schneider), 1801
Habitat Coral reef, rocky reef
Distribution WA
Depth Range 8 to 20 metres
Adult Size 43 centimetres
Food Habit Carnivorous: fish
Use Edible
Occurrence Uncommon

A resident of both mainland and continental islands off north Western Australia, *L. fulvus* is not a well known species and this colour photograph taken in 1971 was the first to be taken in Australia.

The blacktail snapper may be seen in pairs, or as individuals around deep gutters and surge channels where during the day it often resides beneath ledges and in open caves close to the bottom.

In shape and size it looks very similar to *L. russelli* but its bronze colouration, white-edged caudal, soft dorsal, ventral and pelvic fins are distinctive. The flesh is of fair quality.

Blacktail snapper *(L. fulvus)*

Family LUTJANIDAE
Common Name Moses snapper
Scientific Name *Lutjanus russelli* (Bleeker), 1849
Habitat Coral reef, rocky reef
Distribution Qld., NT, WA
Depth Range 5 to 35 metres
Adult Size 50 centimetres
Food Habit Carnivorous: fish, crustaceans
Use Edible
Occurrence Common

Relatively abundant over its entire distribution, the Moses snapper ranges from mainland estuaries to continental islands reefs on the east coast, out to the Great Barrier Reef and the Coral Sea.

Although this species has been observed in large schools, it is more likely to be seen in pairs or small groups. During the day it 'holes up' under ledges or gutters with overhangs, but sometimes remains almost motionless in the current behind a coral head, or reef.

Distinguishing features are the black patch at the base of the pectoral and the yellow pectoral, pelvic and yellow ventral fins the latter being white-edged. The black spot on or above the lateral line may be well defined or just a smudge.

Moses snapper *(L. russelli)*

Family LUTJANIDAE
Common Name Stripey snapper
Scientific Name *Lutjanus carponotatus* (Richardson), 1842
Habitat Coral reef, rocky reef
Distribution Qld., NT, WA
Depth Range 4 to 20 metres
Adult Size 38 centimetres
Food Habit Carnivorous: fish, crustaceans
Use Edible
Occurrence Common

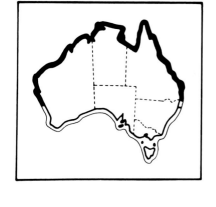

On the east coast where this fish appears to be more common, I have observed it schooling during the day behind large reefs, or hanging in midwater over corals. Sometimes they will take up positions in a coral covered surge channel, but mostly they are seen out in the open. On the North-West Australian coast I failed to find any large schools and those photographed were only in ones and twos and in caves during the day. Their colour varies very little throughout the range, but the number of stripes vary between six and twelve.

An excellent food fish, *L. carponotatus* can be caught by line and taken by trolling over shallow reef areas.

Stripey snapper *(L. carponotatus)*

Family LUTJANIDAE
Common Name Bohar snapper, red bass
Scientific Name *Lutjanus bohar* (Forsskål), 1775
Habitat Coral reef
Distribution Qld., NT, WA
Depth Range 3 to 70 metres
Adult Size 91 centimetres
Food Habit Carnivorous: fish, crustaceans
Use Non-edible
Occurrence Common

Recorded from coastal reefs and continental islands along the north Australian mainland, this snapper is much more prevalent on the northern offshore reefs. In the Coral Sea they are very abundant and a nuisance to line fishermen. They are so numerous throughout the northern part of the Great Barrier Reef that line fishermen must move around continuously to avoid catching them at the exclusion of other more coveted species.

Bohar snapper are territorial and very curious, even to mouthing cameras left on the bottom. Underwater, the fish are a bronze grey colour; when caught, angry, or speared, they turn dark red. They are known to cause ciguatera fish poisoning and therefore should not be eaten. This species has a deep groove in front of each eye.

Bohar snapper *(L. bohar)*

Family LUTJANIDAE
Common Name Hussar
Scientific Name *Lutjanus amabilis* (De Vis), 1885
Habitat Coral reef
Distribution Qld.
Depth Range 8 to 30 metres
Adult Size 45 centimetres
Food Habit Carnivorous: fish, crustaceans
Use Edible
Occurrence Common

The hussar frequents inshore and offshore reefs along the Queensland mainland but is rare in northern areas.

L. amabilis sometimes schools during the day, resting in large caves, or beneath ledges, often in the vicinity of a cleaner fish station. The hussar is a very attractive little snapper, with its bright pink colouration and yellow median stripe, making it easy to identify. It is caught by handline during the day and also at dusk. Due to its small size it is often used for bait by some fishermen though it is quite good eating.

Hussar *(L. amabilis)*

Family LUTJANIDAE
Common Name Red emperor
Scientific Name *Lutjanus sebae* (Cuvier), 1828
Habitat Coral reef
Distribution Qld., NT, WA (also NSW)
Depth Range 15 to 100 metres
Adult Size 1.1 metres
Food Habit Carnivorous: fish
Use Edible
Occurrence Common

Far more prevalent in offshore waters than it is on the mainland, or continental island reefs, the red emperor occurs around coral heads in deeper water where it spends the day hovering close to the bottom.

Adult fish are bronze red with the characteristic darker patches seen on the sub-adult fish still apparent on the top of the soft dorsal, top and bottom of the caudal, and the bottom of the ventral. All fins are white edged except the caudal which has a white stripe. *L. sebae* is often timid underwater, but bites well and fights gamely. This fish is eagerly sought by line fishermen as the flesh is white and of excellent flavour.

Red emperor *(L. sebae)*

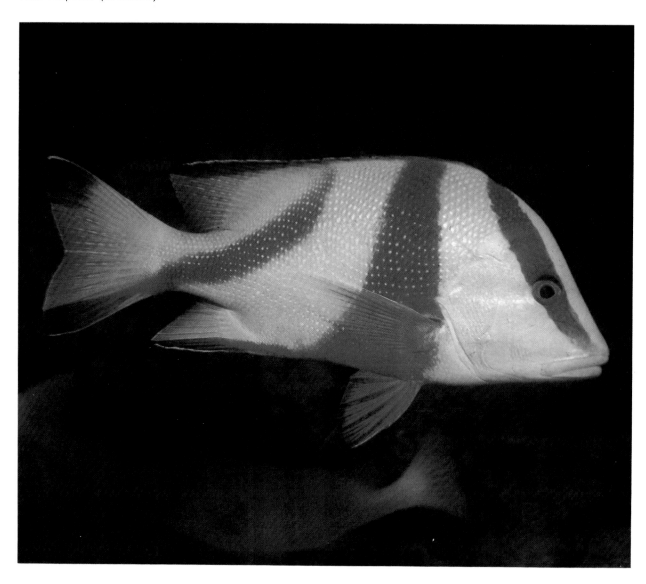

Family LUTJANIDAE
Common Name Paddle-tail
Scientific Name *Lutjanus gibbus* (Forsskål), 1775
Habitat Coral reef
Distribution Qld., NT, WA
Depth Range 5 to 15 metres
Adult Size 60 centimetres
Food Habit Carnivorous: fish
Use Non-edible
Occurrence Common

Paddle-tails are one of the most frustrating species to get close to underwater. One can be in an area where there are hundreds, all milling around in a large school and the closest you can get is ten metres. Even solitary fish are very shy and flighty. They occur on the northern part of the Great Barrier Reef, the Coral Sea and northern Australia. Some fish are seen on the edge of the seaward reefs but the majority are seen in behind the reef in semi-lagoonal situations. Main distinguishing features are the all-black fins trimmed with white, a yellow upper lip, a bright yellow patch at the base of the dorsal and some yellow on the gill cover. The tail is very characteristic, being broad and paddle-like, recurving at the tips. This fish should not be eaten as in some areas it is poisonous.

Paddle-tail *(L. gibbus)*

Family LUTJANIDAE
Common Name Mangrove jack
Scientific Name *Lutjanus argentimaculatus* (Forsskål), 1775
Habitat Coral reef, rocky reef, mangroves
Distribution Qld., NT, WA
Depth Range 1 to 10 metres
Adult Size 1 metre
Food Habit Carnivorous: fish, crustaceans
Use Edible
Occurrence Common

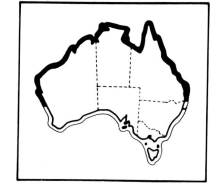

Sometimes it's really difficult to find a particular species of fish to photograph, even when you swim around for hours in all the places they are supposed to be. Such was my experience with the mangrove jack; after years of looking near mangroves, I photographed this one 75 kilometres from the nearest mangrove.

L. argentimaculatus is landed in large quantities by amateur anglers throughout its range, though far more are taken around the mainland reefs and estuaries than from the Great Barrier Reef and Coral Sea.

Mangrove jacks are excellent sport on light gear and are superb eating.

Mangrove jack *(L. argentimaculatus)*

Family LUTJANIDAE
Common Name Black-and-white snapper
Scientific Name *Macolor niger* (Forsskål), 1775
Habitat Coral reef
Distribution Qld., NT, WA
Depth Range 3 to 25 metres
Adult Size 60 centimetres
Food Habit Carnivorous: small fish, invertebrates
Use Edible
Occurrence Uncommon

Macolor niger is a rather unusual snapper, with its rounded forehead, solitary habits and its outer reef edge habitat. In many localities along the Great Barrier Reef and the Coral Sea, *M. niger* can be seen hovering over the edge of 'drop-offs' going down to several hundred feet. As you swim over the edge they come up to meet you, take one look, usually from ten metres away, and flee back into the depths, or away into the many fissures of the reef. Sometimes pairs may be observed and at these times the fish seem much bolder. The common name for this fish only applies to juveniles and sub-adults as mature fish are dark blue with white speckles on the tail and soft dorsal; the other fins are black.

Black-and-white snapper *(M. niger)*

Family CAESIONIDAE
Common Name Scissor-tail fusilier
Scientific Name *Caesio caerulaureus* Lacépède, 1802
Habitat Coral reef
Distribution Qld., NT, WA
Depth Range 2 to 10 metres
Adult Size 27 centimetres
Food Habit Carnivorous: zooplankton
Use Edible
Occurrence Common

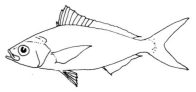

Fusiliers are an interesting but rather confusing group, as similar looking fishes may belong to a different genus, and in some cases a different family. Thanks to research by Dr Gerry Allen, Curator of Fishes at the Western Australian Museum, who is amongst the world's most advanced underwater ichthyologists, we are now in a much better position to identify these fishes correctly.

The scissor-tail fusilier is a gregarious schooling species which inhabits northern areas of the Great Barrier Reef and the Coral Sea. It can be identified by its single broad yellow stripe which runs along the lateral line, and a greenish upper body which runs into the caudal. Each lobe of the tail has a black or dark red streak along it.

Scissor-tail fusilier *(C. caerulaureus)*

Family NEMIPTERIDAE
Common Name Two-line monocle bream
Scientific Name *Scolopsis bilineatus* (Bloch), 1793
Habitat Coral reef, rocky reef
Distribution Qld., NT, WA (also NSW)
Depth Range 3 to 25 metres
Adult Size 22 centimetres
Food Habit Carnivorous: crustaceans
Use Aquarium fish
Occurrence Common

The fishes of this family employ a 'start-stop' type of movement when swimming and that is much more apparent when feeding. *S. bilineatus* is a common little fish which is found on reefs around continental islands and offshore coral reefs and cays. It prefers sheltered waters and is prolific in lagoons and behind the reef proper in the shallow backwaters. The fish itself is very specifically marked and coloured and is easy enough to recognise in the field. Juveniles have black and yellow stripes. They do quite well in aquariums.

Two-line monocle bream (*S. bilineatus*)

Family NEMIPTERIDAE
Common Name Monogrammed monocle bream
Scientific Name *Scolopsis monogramma* (Cuvier and Valenciennes), 1830
Habitat Coral reef, rocky reef, sand, rubble
Distribution Qld., NT, WA
Depth Range 15 to 30 metres
Adult Size 43 centimetres
Food Habit Carnivorous: crustaceans, worms, molluscs
Use Edible
Occurrence Common

By far the largest of the monocle breams, *S. monogramma* occurs throughout the Great Barrier Reef mainland, and continental island reefs. This fish is extremely beautiful and few photographs, or even the imaginative brush of a master painter, have done it justice. Monogrammed monocle bream inhabit areas of sand and sandy rubble along the sheltered drop-offs of back reefs where they meet the sand. It is an active diurnal feeder taking in mouthfuls of sand, extracting the food items and allowing the refuse to filter through the back of the gill plates. The flesh is firm and white but without flavour.

Monogrammed monocle bream *(S. monogramma)*

Family NEMIPTERIDAE
Common Name Latticed monocle bream
Scientific Name *Scolopsis cancellatus* (Cuvier and Valenciennes), 1830
Habitat Coral reef
Distribution Qld.
Depth Range 2 to 10 metres
Adult Size 25 centimetres
Food Habit Carnivorous: crustaceans
Use Aquarium fish
Occurrence Uncommon

Another interesting species, the latticed monocle bream often swims in groups of up to a dozen or so above the reef flats, whereas most other monocle bream have solitary habits.

   S. cancellatus inhabit areas within lagoons, along the reef flats and back edges of reefs, and continental islands. Their colours seem to be stable throughout their distribution. Schools are not easily approached underwater, though solitary specimens seen towards dusk, are.

Latticed monocle bream *(S. cancellatus)*

Family NEMIPTERIDAE
Common Name Pearly monocle bream
Scientific Name *Scolopsis margaritifer* (Cuvier and Valenciennes), 1830
Habitat Coral reef
Distribution Qld.
Depth Range 2 to 15 metres
Adult Size 25 centimetres
Food Habit Carnivorous: crustaceans, molluscs
Use Edible
Occurrence Moderately common

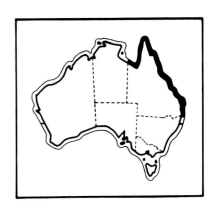

A solitary, coral-dwelling monocle bream, *S. margaritifer* inhabits the Great Barier Reef and the Coral Sea. It is generally territorial and occupies areas where there are one or two sand patches. It can be identified by the presence of pearly spots of blue, silver or yellow on the scales, often forming stripes on the body. There are light blue spots on the cheeks and a light blue stripe running from the nose up over the eye. The fins are translucent blue. It is not commonly caught by line.

Pearly monocle bream *(S. margaritifer)*

Family POMADASYIDAE
Common Name Many-lined sweetlips
Scientific Name *Plectorhynchus multivittatus* (Macleay), 1878
Habitat Coral reef, rocky reef
Distribution Qld., NT, WA
Depth Range 8 to 25 metres
Adult Size 40 centimetres
Food Habit Carnivorous: molluscs
Use Edible
Occurrence Uncommon

At first glance this rather elegant species resembles some snappers which have a similar colour pattern; the rounded profile of the head is unlike that of the snapper.

Many-lined sweetlips appear to be solitary in their habits and, despite their wide distribution, they are rarely observed. They occur near reef clumps and coral heads during the day, usually on the lee side of an island or reef. There is little apparent variation in colour on the few specimens observed.

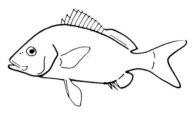

Many-lined sweetlips *(P. multivittatus)*

Family POMADASYIDAE
Common Name Many-spotted sweetlips
Scientific Name *Plectorhynchus chaetodontoides* Lacepede, 1802
Habitat Coral reef, rocky reef
Distribution Qld., NT, WA
Depth Range 4 to 25 metres
Adult Size 60 centimetres
Food Habit Carnivorous: crustaceans, molluscs, fish, algae
Use Edible
Occurrence Common

The common name of this fish is well chosen as it has lots of spots, many of which may be somewhat hexagonal. A very conspicuous species, the many-spotted sweetlips is an inhabitant of mainland reefs, continental island reefs, offshore cays, and true coral island reefs.

By day it hangs in the current in the lee of coral bommies, visits cleaner fish stations on reef surrounds, or groups up with a few others of its kind in a cave, or beneath an overhang. They are a rather tame fish and when resting, are easily speared. The flesh is of fair quality but large fish are dry and rather tasteless.

Many-spotted sweetlips *(P. chaetodontoides)*

Family POMADASYIDAE
Common Name Ribbon sweetlips
Scientific Name *Plectorhynchus polytaenia* (Bleeker), 1852
Habitat Coral reef, rocky reef
Distribution WA, NT
Depth Range 5 to 20 metres
Adult Size 40 centimetres
Food Habit Carnivorous: molluscs, crustaceans
Use Edible
Occurrence Uncommon

The ribbon sweetlips lives on mainland and offshore continental island reefs and prefers protected areas in chasms and caves, where during the day it hovers, moving backwards and forwards in the swell. The juveniles of this species are similar in colour to the adults, but have fewer lines. Ribbon sweetlips can be caught by line and are easily speared due to their disregard of divers. Their flesh, although edible, is not of high quality.

Ribbon sweetlips *(P. polytaenia)*

Family POMADASYIDAE
Common Name Goldman's sweetlips
Scientific Name *Plectorhynchus goldmani* (Bleeker), 1853
Habitat Coral reef, rocky reef
Distribution Qld.
Depth Range 5 to 30 metres
Adult Size 60 centimetres
Food Habit Carnivorous: crustaceans, molluscs
Use Edible
Occurrence Common

Occurring throughout the entire Great Barrier Reef system and the Coral Sea, Goldman's sweetlips are far more prevalent in the northern than southern reefs. Specimens have been encountered on continental island reefs but are exceedingly rare on mainland reefs. As beautiful as this fish is, it is not always easy to get a good photograph, as they are very shy, especially in areas where spearfishing is practised. Although caught by line, very few are landed. The flesh is somewhat coarse, but quite edible.

Goldman's sweetlips *(P. goldmani)*

Family POMADASYIDAE
Common Name Arabian sweetlips
Scientific Name *Plectorhynchus schotaf* (Forsskål), 1775
Habitat Coral reef, rocky reef
Distribution Qld., NT, WA
Depth Range 5 to 20 metres
Adult Size 91 centimetres
Feeding Habit Carnivorous: crustaceans, molluscs
Use Edible
Occurrence Uncommon

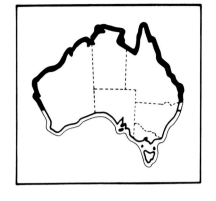

A far-ranging inhabitant of inshore reefs, *P. schotaf* is a rather drab species which when first photographed off north Western Australia in 1971 was unable to be identified alive. Recent expeditions to areas in north Western Australia have provided more specimens and established its identity.

On the Queensland coast it occurs almost down to the New South Wales border. In life, the fish is silver with two black blotches and a black line on the edge of the gill cover; the pectoral fin has a black spot at its base. Juveniles are brownish with black fins.

Arabian sweetlips *(P. schotaf)*

Family POMADASYIDAE
Common Name Harraway's sweetlips
Scientific Name *Plectorhynchus harrawayi* Smith, 1952
Habitat Coral reef, rocky reef
Distribution Qld. (also NSW)
Depth Range 10 to 50 metres
Adult Size 1 metre
Food Habit Carnivorous
Use Edible
Occurrence Common

Only recently identified by Rolly McKay, Harraway's sweetlips has only been seen by a handful of divers, even fewer underwater photographers, this photograph is the first to be published in colour in Australia. Most of the observations on this fish have been on northern reefs of the outer Great Barrier Reef and on one or two of the continental islands. It is a large sweetlips with a very distinctive colour pattern. Juveniles are grey with black fins except for the caudal which is yellow.

Similar to its behaviour underwater in South Africa, this large fish may occur as isolated pairs or on occasions in schools of up to 20, and show very little fear of divers, especially those using scuba in deeper water. The large, white, somewhat grotesque lips are very conspicuous underwater. The flesh of large specimens is coarse and dry.

Harraway's sweetlips *(P. harrawayi)*

Family LETHRINIDAE
Common Name Red-throated emperor
Scientific Name *Lethrinus chrysostomus* Richardson, 1848
Habitat Coral reef
Distribution Qld., WA, NT
Depth Range 5 to 30 metres
Adult Size 1 metre
Food Habit Carnivorous: fish, crustaceans, molluscs
Use Edible
Occurrence Common

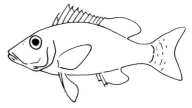

Red-throated emperors form schools during the day and hover over coral or coral heads, sometimes in midwater and sometimes close to the bottom. Some individuals may be seen picking over the substrate around sand and rubble areas where they probe beneath the edges of rocks and in the sand in search of crabs and other prey. At night they move out over the sandy sea floor to feed. Identifying features include a bright red dorsal fin, a red blotch at the base of the pectoral fin, and the inside of the mouth is orange, or red. Common on the southern and central Great Barrier Reef this species is one of the most popular angling and commercial food fish in Queensland.

Red-throated emperor *(L. chrysostomus)*

Family LETHRINIDAE
Common Name Reticulated emperor
Scientific Name *Lethrinus reticulatus* Valenciennes, 1830
Habitat Coral reef, rocky reef
Distribution Qld., NT, WA
Depth Range 1 to 25 metres
Adult Size 40 centimetres
Food Habit Carnivorous: fish, crustaceans, molluscs
Use Edible
Occurrence Common

Not as common, or as large as the red-throated emperor, *L. reticulatus* has a much wider distribution and is recorded from inshore and offshore localities. In some areas this fish does not school during the day and sightings are mainly of individuals. The reticulated emperor is caught by line on fish bait often in association with the red-throated emperor. When excited by bait or burley, both these species go into a feeding frenzy and will bite at anything resembling the bait. This species has red inside the mouth, a pink upper lip, red on the upper pectoral fin, and a yellow patch on top of its eye. Although small, it is good eating.

Reticulated emperor *(L. reticulatus)*

Family LETHRINIDAE
Common Name Naked-headed sea bream
Scientific Name *Gymnocranius griseus* (Temminck and Schlegel), 1843
Habitat Coral reef, sand
Distribution Qld.
Depth Range 5 to 20 metres
Adult Size 50 centimetres
Food Habit Carnivorous: molluscs, crustaceans
Use Edible
Occurrence Moderately common

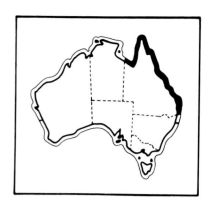

Encountered around sandy lagoons along the outer Great Barrier Reef and cays of the Coral Sea, and occasionally near the mainland, the naked-headed sea bream is usually a solitary animal. It swims a few metres from the bottom, making short forays to the sandy sea floor to investigate any movement which might indicate the presence of prey. *G. griseus* may vary in colour from silvery-white to silvery-pink; has several black streaks on its pectoral, and a very distinctive black eyebrow. This fish will take a fish bait and is good eating.

Naked-headed sea bream *(G. griseus)*

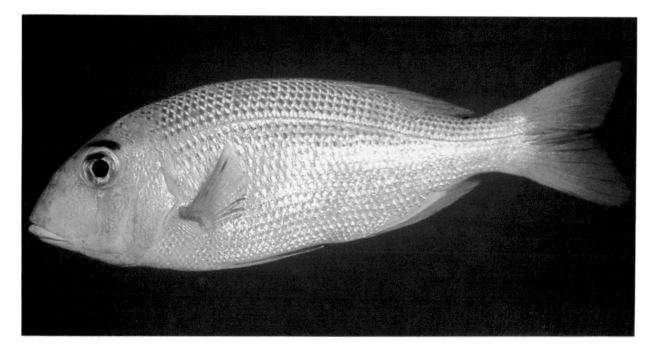

Family LETHRINIDAE
Common Name Collared sea bream
Scientific Name *Gymnocranius bitorquatus* Cockerell, 1916
Habitat Coral reef, sand
Distribution Qld.
Depth Range 5 to 30 metres
Adult Size 40 centimetres
Food Habit Carnivorous: crustaceans, molluscs, worms
Use Edible
Occurrence Common

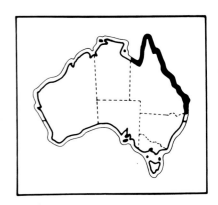

This very distinctive species is prominently marked by a white band formed into a circle, or collar, behind the eye. The collared sea bream is a Great Barrier Reef fish that sometimes occurs on the coast and also in the Coral Sea. It is a diurnal species feeding on areas of broken coral, rubble and sand. *G. bitorquatus* is a solitary species and appears to be territorial. It is commonly handlined and is easy to approach underwater. The flesh is white and palatable, occasionally having an iodine flavour.

Collared sea bream *(G. bitorquatus)*

Family LETHRINIDAE
Common Name Japanese sea bream
Scientific Name *Gymnocranius japonicus* Akazaki, 1962
Habitat Coral reef, sand
Distribution Qld.
Depth Range 10 to 30 metres
Adult Size 50 centimetres
Food Habit Carnivorous: crustaceans, molluscs
Use Edible
Occurrence Common

The Japanese sea bream has been recorded from the outer Great Barrier Reef and the Coral Sea and until a few years ago was unknown in Australian waters. *G. japonicus* may vary in colour from pink to bronze, the body is dappled with dark smudges the majority of which occur below the lateral line, and all fins are edged with white. During the day the Japanese sea bream hovers several metres above the interface between the reef and the sand in sheltered lagoons. It is good eating.

Japanese sea bream *(G. japonicus)*

Family LETHRINIDAE
Common Name Large-eyed sea bream
Scientific Name *Monotaxis grandoculis* (Forsskål), 1775
Habitat Coral reef, sand
Distribution Qld.
Depth Range 10 to 20 metres
Adult Size 76 centimetres
Food Habit Carnivorous: crustaceans, molluscs
Use Edible
Occurrence Common

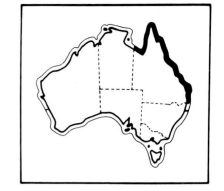

Occurring mainly along the outer northern areas of the Great Barrier Reef, *M. grandoculis* is also found around some of the continental islands from central Queensland north, and is very common in the reef complexes of the Coral Sea. Although it is only a small sea bream, its large eyes, short snout, and three white body bars are diagnostic. Swimming as individuals or in groups, the large-eyed sea bream feeds over sandy coral rubble and broken reef.

Large-eyed sea bream *(M. grandoculis)*

Family MULLIDAE
Common Name Red goatfish
Scientific Name *Parupeneus porphyreus* Jenkins, 1903
Habitat Coral reef
Distribution Qld. (also NSW)
Depth Range 3 to 20 metres
Adult Size 30 centimetres
Food Habit Carnivorous: crustaceans, worms
Use Edible
Occurrence Common

One of Australia's largest goatfish, *P. porphyreus* juveniles are frequently found in large schools. Individuals, pairs and even groups of a dozen, or more, will sometimes mill around cleaner fish stations intermixed with other goatfish. Large adults observed over a three year period are generally solitary and return to the same resting places after early morning feeding. Juveniles are brown on the upper half and orange below, with two prominent white bars running from the snout through the eye to the centre of the back. There is a white spot at the base of the soft dorsal which is prominent on juveniles and adults.

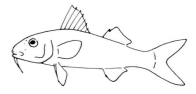

Red goatfish *(P. porphyreus)*

Family MULLIDAE
Common Name Dash-and-dot goatfish
Scientific Name *Parupeneus barberinus* (Lacepede), 1802
Habitat Coral reef, sand
Distribution Qld., NT, WA (also NSW)
Depth Range 5 to 20 metres
Adult Size 50 centimetres
Food Habit Carnivorous: worms, crustaceans, molluscs
Use Edible
Occurrence Moderately common

A large, active diurnal goatfish that swims in small groups of four or five, or as individuals, *P. barberinus* is found in sandy lagoons on offshore islands and cays of the Great Barrier Reef and Coral Sea. Goatfish are the chameleons of the fish world and can change colours and patterns rapidly depending on their mood, the time, or when feeding. It should be stressed that these patterns are not in any way haphazard, each acts as a signal and as such can be photographically recorded. The dash-and-dot goatfish is fairly easy to identify; its black dot is right on the caudal peduncle and quite large. An extremely good eating species.

Dash-and-dot goatfish *(P. barberinus)*

Family MULLIDAE
Common Name Double-bar goatfish
Scientific Name *Parupeneus bifasciatus* (Lacepede), 1802
Habitat Coral reef
Distribution Qld., NT, WA
Depth Range 2 to 60 metres
Adult Size 26 centimetres
Food Habit Carnivorous: crustaceans, worms
Use Edible
Occurrence Moderately common

Like many species of goatfish, *P. bifasciatus* spends the daylight hours resting on the bottom in hollows amongst the coral reef. On some occasions goatfish may rest as a school, all laying down and facing the same direction. When feeding, the double-bar goatfish is usually solitary, and in the early mornings forages in the sand pockets inside lagoons. This fish has a very distinctive colour pattern and has good tasting flesh.

Double-bar goatfish *(P. bifasciatus)*

Family MULLIDAE
Common Name Gold-striped goatfish
Scientific Name *Mulloidichthys vanicolensis* (Valenciennes), 1831
Habitat Coral reefs
Distribution Qld., NT (also NSW)
Depth Range 3 to 20 metres
Adult Size 20 centimetres
Food Habitat Carnivorous: crustaceans, worms
Use Aquarium fish
Occurrence Uncommon

One of the smaller goatfish occurring along the Great Barrier Reef and in the Coral Sea this rather attractive little fish is observed in small groups of up to ten fish. Specimens seen on the reef during the day are either resting, or being cleaned by cleanerfish. Unlike the yellow-lined goatfish *M. flavolineatus*, the gold-striped goatfish has no black spot on the body. Underwater it is easily approached.

Gold-striped goatfish *(M. vanicolensis)*

Family MULLIDAE
Common Name Yellow-lined goatfish
Scientific Name *Mulloidichthys flavolineatus* (Lacépède), 1802
Habitat Coral reef, sand, rocky reef
Distribution Qld., NT, WA (also NSW)
Depth Range 1 to 20 metres
Food Habit Carnivorous: crustaceans, worms
Use Edible
Occurrence Common

Although we have some 22 species of goatfishes in Australian waters, they are little known and while some are difficult to identify, others appear to be simple. *M. flavolineatus* swim in schools near coral and rocky reefs, mostly in offshore waters. During the day they grub for invertebrates in the sand using their long thin barbels to sense their prey. Large adults turn white when feeding on sand and the yellow body stripe may be subdued; the black spot on the centre of the body on the lateral line, is a good distinguishing feature.

Yellow-lined goatfish *(M. flavolineatus)*

143

Family PEMPHERIDAE
Common Name Ransonnet's bullseye
Scientific Name *Parapriacanthus ransonneti* Steindachner, 1870
Habitat Coral reef
Distribution Qld., WA (also NSW)
Depth Range 3 to 15 metres
Adult Size 12 centimetres
Food Habit Carnivorous: crustaceans
Use Aquarium fish
Occurrence Uncommon

A small, elongate, schooling species which inhabits coral reefs in the tropics, these little fish are found during the day beneath ledges, in caves and under overhangs. A school consists of some 30 to 40 closely packed individuals. Recently observed at Lord Howe Island off New South Wales, their colouration during the day is translucent yellowish anteriorly with a bronze tail region. The vertebrae can be seen through the posterior part of the fish's body. Bullseyes hunt at night and feed on small crustaceans.

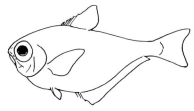

Ransonnet's bullseye *(P. ransonneti)*

Family PEMPHERIDAE
Common Name Bronze bullseye
Scientific Name *Pempheris analis* Waite, 1910
Habitat Coral reef, rocky reef
Distribution Qld., WA (also NSW)
Depth Range 5 to 40 metres
Adult Size 17 centimetres
Food Habit Carnivorous: crustaceans
Use Aquarium fish
Occurrence Common

The bronze bullseye is a nocturnal species, that during the day lives beneath caves and ledges in small groups. If approached too closely it will swim deep into the shelter of the reef.

Bronze bullseyes are residents of inshore mainland reefs, continental island reefs and are common throughout the Great Barrier Reef. They emerge from their caverns sometime after dusk and feed on small crustaceans. There are black tips on the dorsal ventral and caudal fin.

Bronze bullseye *(P. analis)*

Family EPHIPPIDAE
Common Name Pinnate batfish
Scientific Name *Platax pinnatus* (Linnaeus), 1758
Habitat Coral reef, rocky reef
Distribution Qld., NT, WA
Depth Range 8 to 20 metres
Adult Size 50 centimetres
Food Habit Omnivorous: algae
Use Aquarium fish
Occurrence Uncommon

Young *P. pinnatus* live in coral reef areas on continental islands and along the Great Barrier Reef to the Coral Sea. They usually inhabit caves, or live beneath close-lying ledges. Very small ones actually swim on their sides and it has been suggested that they mimic flatworms (inedible polyclad worms). They are extremely popular as aquarium fish and grow up to 30 centimetres before they begin to lose their juvenile colours. Batfish undergo rather remarkable changes in shape with growth.

Pinnate batfish *(P. pinnatus)*. Inset: juvenile

Family EPHIPPIDAE
Common Name Humphead batfish
Scientific Name *Platax batavianus* Cuvier and Valenciennes, 1831
Habitat Coral reef, rocky reef
Distribution Qld., NT, WA
Depth Range 8 to 40 metres
Adult Size 50 centimetres
Food Habit Omnivorous: algae, zooplankton
Use Edible
Occurrence Common

During early morning the humphead batfish move out over the sandy coral rubble bottom and feed on algae. The school later reforms and rest facing up current by waving their fins. Adolescents occur in lagoons and around back reefs, whilst adults may be seen swimming alone or in pairs in surge channels and over exposed reefs. No skill is needed to spear these fish and large specimens are rarely eaten. These fish occur on both mainland and offshore reefs.

Humphead batfish *(P. batavianus)*

Family EPHIPPIDAE
Common Name Round batfish
Scientific Name *Platax orbicularis* (Forsskål), 1775
Habitat Coral reefs
Distribution Qld.
Depth Range 10 to 25 metres
Adult Size 50 centimetres
Food Habit Omnivorous: algae
Use Edible
Occurrence Uncommon

Whereas most adult batfish are solitary, *P. orbicularis* adults sometimes form large schools (up to thirty fish). Juveniles lose their triangular shape with extended dorsal and anal fins, as they mature, and lose the black bars. Round batfish feed over open sand and dead coral rubble throughout the morning, tearing off mouthfuls of filamentous algae with their mouths. Adult fish are uniformly silver with two faint head stripes, dusky pectorals, pelvics, and a faint black edge to other fins. Along the lateral line, and just below the dorsal fin there may be one or two rows of pearly scales. *P. orbicularis* is probably the most palatable of the batfish, but they are as 'tough as tyres'.

Round batfish *(P. orbicularis)*

Family EPHIPPIDAE
Common Name Teira batfish
Scientific Name *Platax teira* (Forsskål), 1775
Habitat Coral reef, rocky reef
Distribution Qld., NT, WA
Depth Range 3 to 20 metres
Adult Size 50 centimetres
Food Habit Omnivorous: algae, salps, sea jellies, zooplankton
Use Edible
Occurrence Common

This large batfish is very common in northern Australia, they swim in groups and may occupy select areas of reef for a long period. They feed during early mornings on filamentous algae. During summer months when sea jellies and salps (pelagic ascidians) are abundant, this species has been seen to prey on these animals. *P. teira* has yellow pelvic fins whilst *P. pinnatus* has black pelvic fins. *P. teira* is easily approached underwater and although edible, is extremely tough and flavourless.

Teira batfish *(P. teira)*

Family CHAETODONTIDAE
Common Name Black-backed butterflyfish
Scientific Name *Chaetodon melannotus* Bloch and Schneider, 1801
Habitat Coral reef, rocky reef
Distribution Qld. (also NSW)
Depth Range 1 to 25 metres
Adult Size 17 centimetres
Food Habit Carnivorous: sessile invertebrates
Use Aquarium fish
Occurrence Common

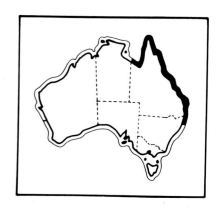

A common fish on the inshore and offshore reefs and islands of eastern Australia, *C. melannotus* may be seen living in lagoons and sheltered waters usually amongst lush coral growth. Similar to many of the smaller butterflyfish this species is easily approached underwater and has little fear of divers. Most of my observations have been on solitary individuals, although pairing is known. The black-backed butterflyfish is active during the day and feeds over a wide area of reef. This fish is easily maintained in aquaria and will accept a variety of natural foods, as well as commercial packet, or frozen food.

Black-backed butterflyfish *(C. melannotus)*

Family CHAETODONTIDAE
Common Name Golden-striped butterflyfish
Scientific Name *Chaetodon aureofasciatus* Macleay, 1878
Habitat Coral reef, rocky reef
Distribution Qld., NT, WA (also NSW)
Depth Range 5 to 15 metres
Adult Size 12.5 centimetres
Food Habit Carnivorous: coral polyps
Use Aquarium fish
Occurrence Common

Ten years ago when I obtained this photograph in north Western Australia, it was not common knowledge that some butterflyfishes feed exclusively on coral polyps and coral mucous. I had spent many hours in the water watching them feed, but it was another thing to photograph the event. The golden-striped butterflyfish was the first species I photographed feeding on live coral polyps and since then I have seen many species doing so. This fish occurs in shallow water on inshore and offshore reefs and although individual fish are seen, pairs, or small groups are most common. Often one or two juveniles will join a pair and are allowed to tag along. This species is difficult to maintain in aquariums.

Golden-striped butterflyfish *(C. aureofasciatus)*

Family CHAETODONTIDAE
Common Name Dusky butterflyfish
Scientific Name *Chaetodon flavirostris* Gunther, 1873
Habitat Coral reef
Distribution Qld. (also NSW)
Depth Range 5 to 15 metres
Adult Size 20 centimetres
Food Habit Carnivorous: worms, sessile invertebrates
Use Aquarium fish
Occurrence Moderately common

Found throughout the Great Barrier Reef, *C. flavirostris* is more abundant on southern reefs. They may be seen in pairs, singularly, or in groups of up to ten individuals. In some areas of the Great Barrier Reef this species inhabits back reefs and may prefer cave situations, feeding beneath the shady recesses of coral bommies. At Lord Howe Island, New South Wales, it is always seen out in the open on sheltered reef slopes, sometimes in large aggregations feeding in open water!

Dusky butterflyfish (*C. flavirostris*)

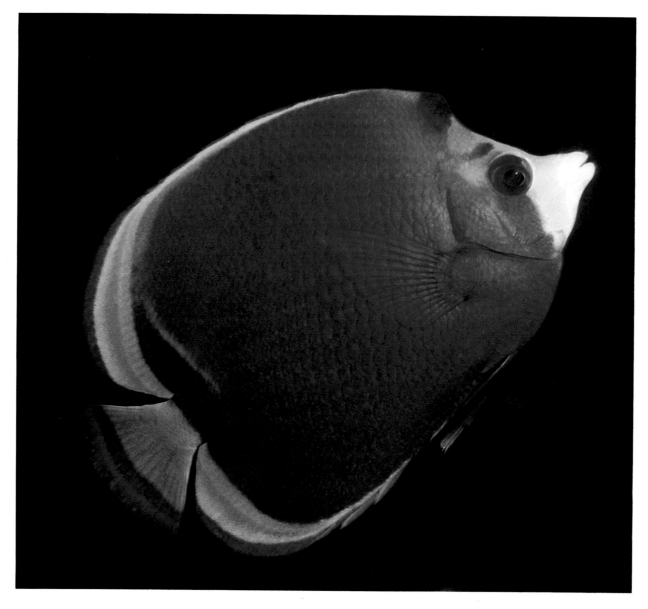

Family CHAETODONTIDAE
Common Name Double-saddle butterflyfish
Scientific Name *Chaetodon ulientensis* Cuvier, 1831
Habitat Coral reef
Distribution Qld., NT. WA
Depth Range 5 to 10 metres
Adult Size 15 centimetres
Food Habit Carnivorous: benthic invertebrates
Use Aquarium fish
Occurrence Uncommon

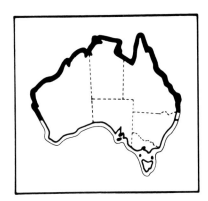

Preferring a habitat of coral slopes, edges of channels within reefs and around bommies beyond backreefs, *C. ulientensis* has a very smooth streamlined look about it. Although much smaller in size, the double-saddle butterflyfish is somewhat similar at first glance to the larger *C. lineatus*. Underwater, *C. ulientensis* is more easily approached than *C. lineatus* and can be distinguished by the bright yellow posterior third of its body, the black spot on the caudal peduncle, the black edge to the tail, and the two dark saddles, as the common name implies. Whereas *C. lineatus* is almost always seen in pairs, often in deeper water *C. ulientensis* is regularly observed as individuals.

Double-saddle butterflyfish *(C. ulientensis)*

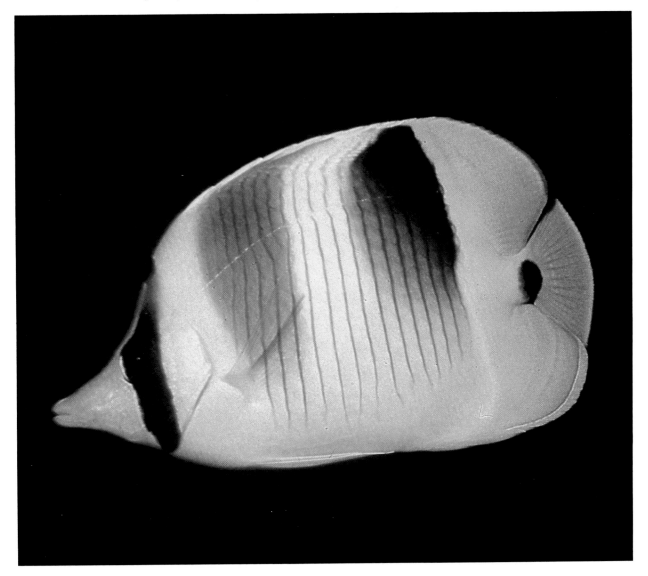

Family CHAETODONTIDAE
Common Name Striped butterflyfish
Scientific Name *Chaetodon trifasciatus* Park, 1797
Habitat Coral reef, rocky reef
Distribution Qld., NT, WA (also NSW)
Depth Range 1 to 15 metres
Adult Size 12 centimetres
Food Habit Carnivorous: coral polyps
Use Aquarium fish
Occurrence Common

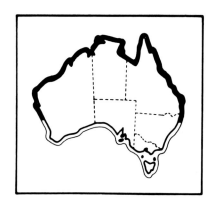

The striped butterflyfish is common in rich coral areas around back reefs, bommies, reef flats and in sheltered lagoons. They are always seen in pairs and are more common in shallow water than deeper. Non territorial fishes, I have followed a pair for several hundred metres along a reef and they were still going away when I gave up. The striped butterflyfish browses on coral polyps and for this reason it is best to introduce juveniles to a tank and train them to take other food.

Striped butterflyfish (*C. trifasciatus*)

Family CHAETODONTIDAE
Common Name Klein's butterflyfish
Scientific Name *Chaetodon kleini* Bloch, 1790
Habitat Coral reef, rocky reef
Distribution Qld. (also NSW)
Depth Range 5 to 20 metres
Adult Size 12 centimetres
Food Habit Carnivorous: sessile invertebrates, worms
Use Aquarium fish
Occurrence Common

Klein's butterflyfish is common on the northern area of the Great Barrier Reef and the reefs and cays of the Coral Sea. It is usually seen alone, although pairs have been sighted during summer. Fairly easy to approach underwater, it picks around live coral, coraline algae, and dead coral. *C. kleini* lives in calm waters, in lagoons, behind reefs, and near islands. Klein's butterflyfish is a hardy aquarium fish.

Klein's butterflyfish *(C. kleini)*

Family CHAETODONTIDAE
Common Name Bennett's butterflyfish
Scientific Name *Chaetodon bennetti* (Cuvier), 1831
Habitat Coral reef
Distribution Qld. (also NSW)
Depth Range 1 to 10 metres
Adult Size 15 centimetres
Food Habit Carnivorous: coral polyps and mucous
Use Aquarium fish
Occurrence Not common

Bennett's butterflyfish seems to be far more prevalent on the northern Great Barrier Reef than it does on the mainland and offshore reefs of the southern Great Barrier Reef. *C. bennetti* is an exceedingly shy species and one must employ all sorts of devious 'fish tricks' underwater in order to get close enough for a good photograph. This species is solitary and diurnal, feeding exclusively on coral polyps and mucous. It is not easy to maintain in aquaria due to its rather specialised natural diet.

Bennett's butterflyfish *(C. bennetti)*

Family CHAETODONTIDAE
Common Name Baronessa butterflyfish
Scientific Name *Chaetodon baronessa* (Cuvier and Valenciennes), 1831
Habitat Coral reef, rocky reef
Distribution Qld. (also NSW)
Depth Range 3 to 10 metres
Adult Size 15 centimetres
Food Habit Carnivorous: coral polyps
Use Aquarium fish
Occurrence Common

An easily identified little butterflyfish, *C. baronessa* inhabits the Great Barrier Reef and the Coral Sea. Adults are usually seen in pairs around back reefs, bommies, on the reef flats, reef slopes, and in sheltered lagoons. They appear to be very selective in their choice of polyps and are continually on the move, rarely showing interest in anything but staghorn corals. The baronessa butterflyfish is very shy and elusive and is not easy to maintain under aquarium conditions.

Baronessa butterflyfish *(C. baronessa)*

Family CHAETODONTIDAE
Common Name Gunther's butterflyfish
Scientific Name *Chaetodon guntheri* Ahl, 1913
Habitat Rocky reef, coral reef
Distribution NSW
Depth Range 5 to 33 metres
Adult Size 15 centimetres
Food Habit Carnivorous: benthic invertebrates
Use Aquarium fish
Occurrence Uncommon

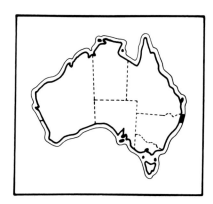

Very similar to *C. citrinellus,* Gunther's butterflyfish has so far only been recorded from Lord Howe Island and the New South Wales mainland almost to the Queensland border. It can be separated from *C. citrinellus* by the intense yellow band which runs around the rear of the body of *C. guntheri,* from the centre of the soft dorsal down to the ventral fin. *C. guntheri* has only a thin black line running around the outside edge of the yellow band, which is edged with white. *C. citrinellus* has a deep black edge to its anal fin. Gunther's butterflyfish is almost always seen alone, whether in shallow water or at depth.

Gunther's butterflyfish *(C. guntheri)*

Family CHAETODONTIDAE
Common Name Racoon butterflyfish
Scientific Name *Chaetodon lunula* (Lacépède), 1802
Habitat Coral reef, rocky reef
Distribution Qld., NT, WA (also NSW)
Depth Range 5 to 25 metres
Adult Size 17 centimetres
Food Habit Carnivorous: coral polyps, molluscs, worms
Use Aquarium fish
Occurrence Common

This is a popular aquarium species living in a variety of habitats around inshore and offshore reefs. Often found in both sheltered and exposed areas, especially near the undersides of caves and coral heads where during the day it swims close to the encrusted walls. *C. lunula* may also be active during the night as I have never found one asleep during night-diving excursions. Most observations show the racoon butterflyfish to be solitary, though at some locations pairs have been seen. It is also known to school at certain times.

Racoon butterflyfish *(C. lunula)*

Family CHAETODONTIDAE
Common Name Threadfin butterflyfish
Scientific Name *Chaetodon auriga* (Forsskål), 1775
Habitat Coral reef, rocky reef
Distribution Qld., NT, WA (also NSW)
Depth Range 1 to 20 metres
Adult Size 22 centimetres
Food Habit Carnivorous: worms, crustaceans
Use Aquarium fish
Occurrence Common

There are a number of butterflyfish similar to *C. auriga* found throughout the waters of tropical Australia, but the adults of this species can be easily identified by the long thread-like filament extending from the soft dorsal, and the black ocellus directly below. The body stripes, sloped towards the ventral fin, may be disrupted in some specimens. *C. auriga* is easily approached underwater and will accept captivity rather well if maintained in a large tank.

Threadfin butterflyfish *(C. auriga)*

Family CHAETODONTIDAE
Common Name Vagabond butterflyfish
Scientific Name *Chaetodon vagabundus* (Linnaeus), 1758
Habitat Coral reef, rocky reef
Distribution Qld. (also NSW)
Depth Range 5 to 25 metres
Adult Size 20 centimetres
Food Habit Carnivorous: worms, sessile invertebrates
Use Aquarium fish
Occurrence Common

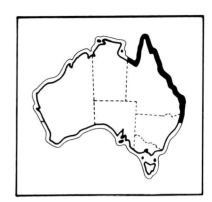

Somewhat similar in colour pattern to *C. auriga*, the vagabond butterflyfish can be easily separated by the black bar on the soft dorsal running down through the caudal peduncle. This fish lives on inshore and offshore reefs and juveniles have even been found in mainland rivers. Underwater, the vagabond butterflyfish is easy to approach and may be seen singly, or in pairs. It prefers sheltered waters in lagoons or behind back reefs and has a fairly unrestricted diet. *C. vagabundus* make good pets and will accept captivity with minimum requirements of a large well-balanced tank.

Vagabond butterflyfish *(C. vagabundus)*

Family CHAETODONTIDAE
Common Name Blue-spot butterflyfish
Scientific Name *Chaetodon plebeius* Cuvier, 1831
Habitat Coral reef, rocky reef
Distribution Qld., WA (also NSW)
Depth Range 1 to 10 metres
Adult Size 12 centimetres
Food Habit Carnivorous: benthic invertebrates, algae
Use Aquarium fish
Occurrence Common

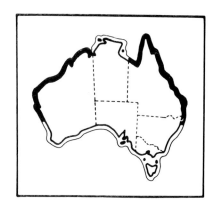

A resident of sheltered, shallow water lagoons and back reefs along the Great Barrier Reef in inshore and offshore areas this fish is also found at Lord Howe Island. *C. plebeius* has a unique easily-recognisable colouration, as do many members of this family. They are easy to approach underwater and become accustomed to divers very quickly. Blue-spot butterflyfish swim in pairs and there appears to be very little colour variation in adult fishes. With proper upkeep this species lives well in medium-sized aquaria.

Blue-spot butterflyfish *(C. plebeius)*

Family CHAETODONTIDAE
Common Name Chevroned butterflyfish
Scientific Name *Chaetodon trifascialis* Quoy and Gaimard, 1824
Habitat Coral reef
Distribution Qld., NT, WA (also NSW)
Depth Range 2 to 10 metres
Adult Size 18 centimetres
Food Habit Carnivorous: coral polyps
Use Aquarium fish
Occurrence Common

This highly territorial butterflyfish is only found on or around a tabular colony of staghorn coral in shallow water. In some very rich coral areas where several formations of tabular coral overlap or terrace, *C. trifascialis* may allow a few butterflyfish into its territory, but otherwise will chase away all other coral-eating butterflyfishes. Due to its territorial behaviour the fish can be easily photographed. It is unlikely to do well under aquarium conditions.

Chevroned butterflyfish *(C. trifascialis)*

Family CHAETODONTIDAE
Common Name Saddled butterflyfish
Scientific Name *Chaetodon ephippium* Cuvier and Valenciennes, 1831
Habitat Coral reef, rocky reef
Distribution Qld., WA (also NSW)
Depth Range 5 to 15 metres
Adult Size 25 centimetres
Food Habit Carnivorous: algae, worms, coral polyps
Use Aquarium fish
Occurrence Moderately common

This spectacular butterflyfish inhabits lagoons and inner reef areas and is often found on the edge of reef slopes and channels. *C. ephippium* is usually seen in pairs and is sometimes difficult to approach, being somewhat wary of divers. It appears to be more numerous on the Great Barrier Reef than in north Western Australia and, unlike some other butterflyfish, the juvenile's colour pattern is similar to that of the adult. This fish needs a large tank and lots of care in feeding.

Saddled butterflyfish *(C. ephippium)*

Family CHAETODONTIDAE
Common Name Merten's butterflyfish
Scientific Name *Chaetodon mertensii* Cuvier and Valenciennes, 1831
Habitat Coral reef
Distribution Qld. (also NSW)
Depth Range 8 to 20 metres
Adult Size 15 centimetres
Food Habit Carnivorous: small invertebrates, algae
Use Aquarium fish
Occurrence Uncommon

A rather timid little fish found on the outer northern reefs, in the Coral Sea and at Lord Howe Island off New South Wales, Merten's butterflyfish makes an excellent aquarium pet. It is observed on back reefs and in lagoon situations. A loose pair bond is formed during summer but most are seen as individual fish. The first records in Australian waters were only noticed within the last ten years, from off Cairns. This species is less timid when found in deeper waters of 15 to 20 metres.

Merten's butterflyfish *(C. mertensii)*

Family CHAETODONTIDAE
Common Name Meyer's butterflyfish
Scientific Name *Chaetodon meyeri* Bloch and Schneider, 1801
Habitat Coral reef
Distribution Qld., WA
Depth Range 10 to 15 metres
Adult Size 20 centimetres
Food Habit Carnivorous: coral polyps
Use Aquarium fish
Occurrence Rare

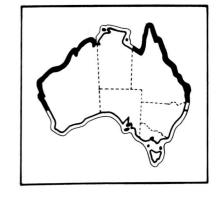

First recorded in Australian waters by underwater photographer Roger Steene, Meyer's butterflyfish lives in outer reef areas along the Great Barrier Reef and in the Coral Sea.

This fish has only been observed singly, however it will swim around with paired specimens of *C. ornatissimus*. *C. meyeri* frequents drop offs and outer reef faces, where it forages during the day along the walls and in cave complexes. It is difficult to get close to and to obtain a good photograph one must lie in ambush.

Meyer's butterflyfish *(C. meyeri)*

Family CHAETODONTIDAE
Common Name Speckled butterflyfish
Scientific Name *Chaetodon citrinellus* Cuvier, 1831
Habitat Coral reef, rocky reef
Distribution Qld., NT, WA (also NSW)
Depth Range 1 to 10 metres
Adult Size 12 centimetres
Food Habit Carnivorous: benthic invertebrates, worms
Use Aquarium fish
Occurrence Common

The speckled butterflyfish is a common species found frequently in sheltered lagoon habitats. Sometimes solitary, but usually in pairs, the speckled butterflyfish is seen on inshore and offshore reefs and around continental islands. It can be easily approached underwater and shows little fear of divers, or other butterflyfish, and is more intolerant of other species when paired. Body colouration appears to intensify with maturity; the smaller fish having a much lighter body colour than larger ones which can be almost gold.

Speckled butterflyfish *(C. citrinellus)*

Family CHAETODONTIDAE
Common Name Ornate butterflyfish
Scientific Name *Chaetodon ornatissimus* Cuvier, 1831
Habitat Coral reef, rocky reef
Distribution Qld., WA
Depth Range 8 to 25 metres
Adult Size 17 centimetres
Food Habit Carnivorous: coral polyps, coral mucous
Use Aquarium fish
Occurrence Moderately common

Although the ornate butterflyfish had been recorded from the Great Barrier Reef for many years, its presence in Western Australia was unknown until my Australian coastal marine expedition in 1971, when photographs of this beautiful fish were taken. It swims in pairs, singularly or in small groups in exposed areas around offshore islands, slopes and terraces of outer reefs, and also in lagoons. This fish is not easily kept in aquaria, though I know several people who have managed, through sheer perserverance.

Ornate butterflyfish *(C. ornatissimus)*

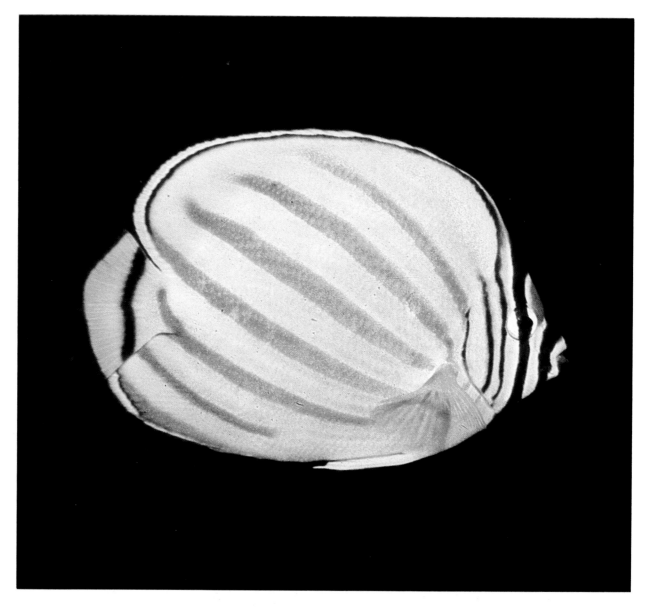

Family CHAETODONTIDAE
Common Name Reticulated butterflyfish
Scientific Name *Chaetodon reticulatus* (Smith), 1952
Habitat Coral reef
Distribution Qld.
Depth Range 1 to 40 metres
Adult Size 15 centimetres
Food Habit Carnivorous: invertebrates
Use Aquarium fish
Occurrence Uncommon

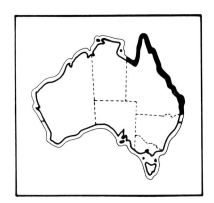

A rare and rather beautiful species, the reticulated butterflyfish inhabits both shallow and deep waters and is mostly seen in the vicinity of sloping reef faces along the outer Great Barrier Reef and around the sides of giant coral heads in the Coral Sea. This species appears to favour the overhangs and undersides of drop-off walls rather than rich coral habitats.

Reticulated butterflyfish *(C. reticulatus)*

Family CHAETODONTIDAE
Common Name Rainford's butterflyfish
Scientific Name *Chaetodon rainfordi* McCulloch, 1923
Habitat Coral reef
Distribution Qld. (also NSW)
Depth Range 1 to 20 metres
Adult Size 12 centimetres
Food Habit Carnivorous: invertebrates, algae
Use Aquarium fish
Occurrence Moderately common

Due to the bright yellow body and orange stripes this small butterflyfish is very conspicuous when seen in the clear waters of tropical lagoons. This species is restricted to the Great Barrier Reef and Lord Howe Island. It swims singly or in pairs and prefers the quiet coral rich areas of back reef and lagoonal reef flats. *C. rainfordi* is a 'dainty' eater, as it is very selective and only takes what appears to be a minute amount of food at each pick. It is kept successfully in aquaria.

Rainford's butterflyfish *(C. rainfordi)*

Family CHAETODONTIDAE
Common Name Long-nosed butterflyfish
Scientific Name *Forcipiger flavissimus* Jordan and McGregor, 1898
Habitat Coral reef, rocky reef
Distribution Qld., NT, WA (also NSW)
Depth Range 8 to 25 metres
Adult Size 12 centimetres
Food Habit Carnivorous: sessile invertebrates, coral polyps
Use Aquarium fish
Occurrence Common

The long-nosed butterflyfish is found on coral reefs on the east coast and in limestone caverns in north Western Australia. It is generally observed in pairs and with a little patience, one can get close enough for a picture. This fish has a beak similar to needle-nose pliers, adapted to tearing pieces from benthic invertebrates. It makes a very fine pet in aquaria.

Long-nosed butterflyfish *(F. flavissimus)*

171

Family CHAETODONTIDAE
Common Name Longer-nosed butterflyfish
Scientific Name *Forcipiger longirostris* (Broussonet), 1782
Habitat Coral reef
Distribution Qld.
Depth Range 8 to 25 metres
Adult Size 18 centimetres
Food Habit Carnivorous: crustaceans
Use Aquarium fish
Occurrence Rare

F. longirostris, like its close relative *F. flavissimus*, has only been seen on the outer areas of the Great Barrier Reef and Coral Sea where it inhabits caves and underledge areas on reef slopes and drop offs. It is easy to get close to, but difficult to get a good photograph due to its contrasting colours and the dark places it frequents. Also, unlike its relative, the diet of the longer-nosed butterflyfish is made up almost entirely of small shrimps and a few crabs. An easy way to separate the two species is to mentally measure the distance between the end of the snout and the back edge of the black facemask; *C. flavissimus* has the front edge of the eye almost central whereas *C. longirostris* has a snout half as long again.

Longer-nosed butterflyfish *(F. longirostris)*

Family CHAETODONTIDAE
Common Name Pyramid butterflyfish
Scientific Name *Hemitaurichthys polylepis* (Bleeker), 1857
Habitat Coral reef
Distribution Qld.
Depth Range 10 to 25 metres
Adult Size 15 centimetres
Food Habit Carnivorous: zooplankton, algae, crustaceans
Use Aquarium fish
Occurrence Common

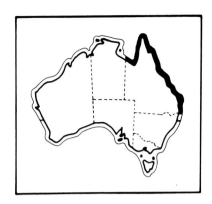

As this fish dwells on the edge of drop-offs along the outer northern edge of the Great Barrier Reef and the isolated giant bommies behind the Coral Sea reefs, the average diver has little opportunity to see *H. polylepis*. This unmistakable species schools and it is quite an experience to drift slowly down the edge of a drop-off through hundreds of little three-colour gems cavorting below. Most of its food consists of larval marine life taken as it drifts by on the current. Perhaps because of this feeding behaviour they are easily fed on packet fish food. They are best maintained under aquarium conditions in groups of three or more.

Pyramid butterflyfish *(H. polylepis)*

Family CHAETODONTIDAE
Common Name Masked bannerfish
Scientific Name *Heniochus monoceros* Cuvier and Valenciennes, 1831
Habitat Coral reef
Distribution Qld. (also NSW)
Depth Range 8 to 25 metres
Adult Size 20 centimetres
Food Habit Carnivorous: benthic invertebrates
Use Aquarium fish
Occurrence Moderately common

Frequently seen throughout the entire Great Barrier Reef system, this species has a wide geographic distribution. A large and conspicuous member of the family, it is generally seen in gutters and reef fissures and also around underwater caves and grottoes where it feeds on animals and invertebrates encrusting the walls. This species alters little in colour pattern during its transition from juvenile to adult and older specimens have a protuberance resembling a short horn just above the eyes. Underwater *H. monoceros* is easily approached. At night it sleeps in holes and cracks in cave roofs and in crevices.

Masked bannerfish *(H. monoceros)*

Family CHAETODONTIDAE
Common Name Schooling bannerfish
Scientific Name *Heniochus diphreutes* Jordan, 1903
Habitat Coral reef, rocky reef
Distribution Qld., WA (also NSW)
Depth Range 5 to 25 metres
Adult Size 20 centimetres
Food Habit Carnivorous
Use Aquarium fish
Occurrence Common

It's interesting to note that for quite some time there was only thought to be one long-fin bannerfish, *H. acuminatus* (see *Australian Sea Fishes South 30°S*). Then, due to investigations by underwater ichthyologist Rudie Kuiter, another species was found. At the time it was assumed to be new but further investigation by Dr Gerry Allen, Curator of Fishes at Western Australian Museum, proved it to be the long lost species, *H. diphreutes*. Although the two fishes behave differently (*H. acuminatus* swimming in pairs and singularly and *H. diphreutes* mostly seen in schools) they are to the casual observer remarkably similar; *H. diphreutes* has an extra dorsal spine. Underwater they can be separated by the second body band, in *H. acuminatus* the black band runs across the caudal peduncle and onto the tail, in *H. diphreutes* it runs down the body and onto the ventral fin missing the junction of the soft caudal with the caudal peduncle.

Schooling bannerfish *(H. diphreutes)*

Family CHAETODONTIDAE
Common Name Pennant bannerfish
Scientific Name *Heniochus chrysostomus* Cuvier and
Valenciennes, 1831
Habitat Coral reef, rocky reef
Distribution Qld., NT, WA (also NSW)
Depth Range 1 to 25 metres
Adult Size 15 centimetres
Food Habit Carnivorous: benthic invertebrates
Use Aquarium fish
Occurrence Uncommon

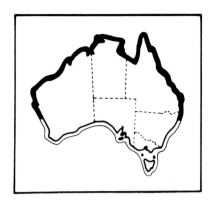

I consider the pennant bannerfish to be the most appealing of all the bannerfishes and one most easy to identify. There is very little variation in pattern, and underwater this species is anything but shy. It occurs in sheltered lagoons, around back reefs and along the slopes of channels between reefs, throughout the Great Barrier Reef and in the Coral Sea. It prefers areas of rich coral growth where there is a lot of broken bottom, affording lots of cover. *H. chrysostomus* does well in a large aquarium.

Pennant bannerfish *(H. chrysostomus)*

Family CHAETODONTIDAE
Common Name Orange-banded coralfish
Scientific Name *Coradion chrysozonus* (Cuvier), 1831
Habitat Coral reef, rocky reef
Distribution Qld., WA, NT
Depth Range 10 to 35 metres
Adult Size 15 centimetres
Food Habit Carnivorous: invertebrates
Use Aquarium fish
Occurrence Uncommon

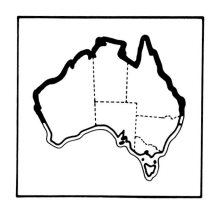

These little fishes seem to prefer deeper waters around back reefs and coral bommies where they spend the day picking at invertebrates in the marine growth on cave walls, and around the bases of coral clumps. On occasion, pairs have been observed to range over an area of 30 to 40 metres. They also occur on broken bottom in moderately deep water. At night, orange-banded coralfishes sleep in crevices in the coral caves. This species is fairly easy to approach underwater and is easily maintained in aquaria.

Orange-banded coralfish *(C. chrysozonus)*

Family CHAETODONTIDAE
Common Name High-fin coralfish
Scientific Name *Coradion altivelis* McCulloch, 1916
Habitat Coral reef, rocky reef
Distribution Qld.
Depth Range 8 to 25 metres
Adult Size 15 centimetres
Food Habit Carnivorous: invertebrates
Use Aquarium fish
Occurrence Uncommon

The high-fin coralfish is somewhat similar to the orange-banded coralfish, but is easily distinguished by its high dorsal fin and the lack of a black ocellus on the rear of the soft dorsal of adults; the juveniles have a large ocellus on the soft dorsal that is lost at maturity. *C. altivelis* occurs on Queensland mainland reefs, around some continental islands, and in the southern and central areas of the Great Barrier Reef. It is easy to maintain in marine aquaria.

High-fin coralfish (*C. altivelis*)

Family CHAETODONTIDAE
Common Name Margined coralfish
Scientific Name *Chelmon marginalis* Richardson, 1842
Habitat Coral reef, rocky reef
Distribution Qld., NT, WA
Depth Range 1 to 30 metres
Adult Size 12 centimetres
Food Habit Carnivorous: invertebrates
Use Aquarium fish
Occurrence Common

The intense colouration of this attractive and interesting fish is magnificent. It is common in many areas but most abundant in north Western Australia. They are usually seen in pairs, although up to five have been seen foraging together. They use their long beaks to tear off pieces of sessile invertebrates, the heads of tube worms and to probe in between coral branches. These fish inhabit mainland reefs, around continental islands and also the northern areas of the Great Barrier Reef. Similar to the close relation, *C. rostratus*, they are popular aquarium fish.

Margined coralfish *(C. marginalis)*

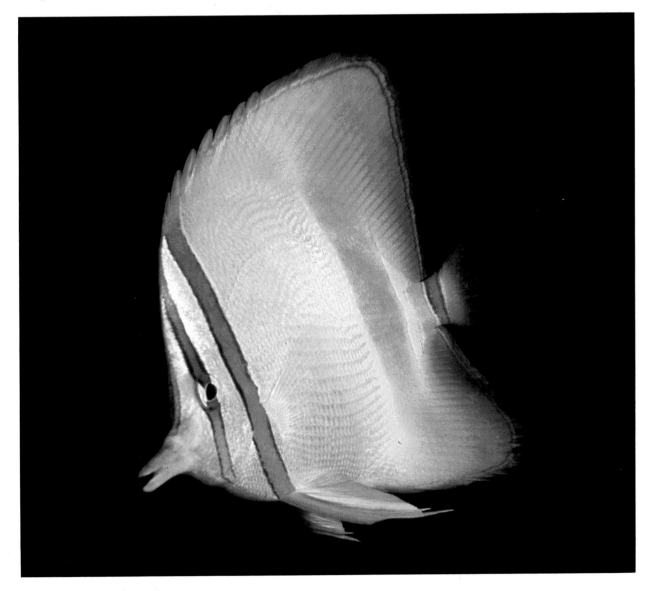

Family CHAETODONTIDAE
Common Name Beaked coralfish
Scientific Name *Chelmon rostratus* (Linnaeus), 1758
Habitat Coral reef, rocky reef
Distribution Qld., NT, WA (also NSW)
Depth Range 1 to 25 metres
Adult Size 16 centimetres
Food Habit Carnivorous: invertebrates
Use Aquarium fish
Occurrence Common

This species has a bright yellow body-band and the adults retain the ocellus on the soft dorsal. The beaked coralfish is common in Northern Australia and occurs on mainland, continental islands and offshore reefs. *C. rostratus* forms pair relationships and sometimes several smaller fishes may accompany them. They use their long beaks to feed on sessile invertebrates and to explore fissures and holes in the reef. Very successful as an aquarium fish, providing a matched pair is obtained and the aquarium a large one.

Beaked coralfish (*C. rostratus*)

Family POMACANTHIDAE
Common Name Blue angelfish
Scientific Name *Pomacanthus semicirculatus* (Cuvier), 1831
Habitat Coral reef, rocky reef
Distribution Qld., NT, WA (also NSW)
Depth Range 5 to 25 metres
Adult Size 38 centimetres
Food Habit Carnivorous: encrusting sessile organisms
Use Aquarium fish
Occurrence Common

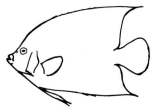

By far the most photographed angelfish in tropical Australia, *P. semicirculatus* is found throughout the Great Barrier Reef where it is more abundant than in north Western Australia. It lives below the reef edge in sheltered lagoons and backreefs and also inhabits continental reefs which are open to surge. During the day it roams through its territory feeding on sponges, ascidians and algae it scrapes from the walls of caves and overhangs with its brush-like teeth. Juveniles can be kept in community aquaria but adults are very territorial and will continually harass other angels or fish of similar feeding habits.

Blue angelfish *(P. semicirculatus)*. Inset: juvenile

Family POMACANTHIDAE
Common Name Emperor angelfish
Scientific Name *Pomacanthus imperator* (Bloch), 1787
Habitat Coral reef, rocky reef
Distribution Qld., NT, WA (also NSW)
Depth Range 10 to 25 metres
Adult Size 38 centimetres
Food Habit Carnivorous: encrusting sessile organisms
Use Aquarium fish
Occurrence Moderately common

In north Western Australia the emperor angelfish lives on mainland reefs and around continental islands; on the east coast most are on the Great Barrier Reef and around a few of the more northern continental islands. Emperor angelfish are territorial and are often seen in caves and grotto complexes on the edges of reef slopes, gutters and surge channel overhangs. As is common with many of the larger angelfish, the juvenile of this species is dark blue, with white markings forming a ring on the back of the body. These fish make exquisite pets, but care must be taken to ensure that they are not placed with conspecifics, or other large angelfish, as they fight.

Emperor angelfish *(P. imperator)*

Family POMACANTHIDAE
Common Name Scribbled angelfish
Scientific Name *Chaetodontoplus duboulayi* (Günther), 1867
Habitat Coral reef, rocky reef
Distribution Qld., NT, WA
Depth Range 3 to 30 metres
Adult Size 30 centimetres
Food Habit Carnivorous: encrusting sessile organisms
Use Aquarium fish
Occurrence Uncommon

This fish is usually restricted to mainland and continental island reefs where it can be found as individuals, or in small groups. In deeper water, *C. duboulayi* may be approached in the open; in shallow waters on the mainland fringing reefs, it is generally seen in shallow caves and under-hangings. This angelfish is sometimes taken by trawl net on prawning grounds at night far from reef and is associated with sponges. Similar to other angelfish *C. duboulayi* is territorial and once the extent of the terri-torial limits are known a diver is able to use the fish's behaviour and inquisitive nature to get close enough to observe, or photograph. The scribbled angelfish does very well in large aquaria.

Scribbled angelfish *(C. duboulayi)*

Family POMACANTHIDAE
Common Name Navarchus angelfish
Scientific Name *Euxiphipops navarchus* (Cuvier), 1831
Habitat Coral reef
Distribution WA
Depth Range 10 to 30 metres
Adult Size 25 centimetres
Food Habit Omnivorous: encrusting organisms
Use Aquarium fish
Occurrence Rare

The navarchus angelfish has been recorded from a sighting at Rowley Shoals off Western Australia. Observations at Port Moresby, Papua New Guinea indicate that *E. navarchus* is a solitary species, though pairs have been seen during early summer. Although specimens are sometimes observed on the edges of drop-offs in shallow water, most fish seem to prefer a deeper water habitat around protected and exposed reefs where they frequent caves, deep underhangs and reef slopes on drop-offs adjacent to deep water.

Navarchus angelfish *(E. navarchus)*

Family POMACANTHIDAE
Common Name Six-banded angelfish
Scientific Name *Euxiphipops sexstriatus* (Cuvier), 1831
Habitat Coral reef, rocky reef
Distribution Qld., NT, WA
Depth Range 5 to 25 metres
Adult Size 50 centimetres
Food Habit Carnivorous: encrusting sessile organisms
Use Edible
Occurrence Common

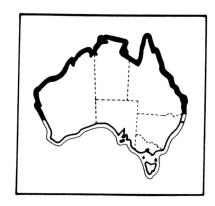

This is the largest angelfish inhabiting the waters of Australia, and is one of the most common. Unlike others of its family, adult six-banded angelfish are not highly territorial, and paired fish are often seen roaming over quite extensive areas of reef. On the other hand, juveniles and some individual fish have been observed in the one small area on numerous occasions. This angelfish tends to inhabit offshore and fringing reefs around continental islands in Western Australia; on the east coast it occurs throughout the entire Great Barrier Reef. The six-banded angelfish is easily approached and shows little fear of divers.

Six-banded angelfish *(E. sexstriatus)*

Family POMACANTHIDAE
Common Name Yellow-faced angelfish
Scientific Name *Euxiphipops xanthometapon* (Bleeker), 1853
Habitat Coral reef
Distribution Qld., WA, NT
Depth Range 5 to 25 metres
Adult Size 38 centimetres
Food Habit Omnivorous: sessile encrusting organisms
Use Aquarium fish
Occurrence Rare

The almost unbelievable colours of the yellow-faced angelfish are just another extraordinary example of nature's underwater extravaganza. Only a few divers in Australia have even had the pleasure of seeing this fish in its natural environment as it lives on the northern reaches of the Great Barrier Reef and inhabits the outer reef fronts. It lives in deep surge gutters and along the edges of broken crevasses and generally retreats into a cave or ledge when threatened. I have only seen this species a couple of times and these were individual fish, both of which were very shy and nervous. On rare occasions *E. xanthometapon* are captured off Cape Moreton near Brisbane.

Yellow-faced angelfish *(E. xanthometapon)*

Family POMACANTHIDAE
Common Name Two-spined angelfish
Scientific Name *Centropyge bispinosus* (Günther), 1860
Habitat Coral reef, rocky reef
Distribution Qld. (also NSW)
Depth Range 5 to 10 metres
Adult Size 12 centimetres
Food Habit Omnivorous: encrusting organisms, algae
Use Aquarium fish
Occurrence Moderately common

In areas of broken dead coral reef surrounded by stands of staghorn coral, this fish occupies a territory which contains a number of escape holes. It is often seen in pairs and sometimes singularly, though in every case it stays close to the reef. This shy behaviour makes the fish extremely difficult to get close to and in many cases the photographs taken are hardly worthwhile. The two-spined angelfish is very common on the Great Barrier Reef and around continental islands. It fares well in aquariums.

Two-spined angelfish *(C. bispinosus)*

Family POMACANTHIDAE
Common Name Multi-barred angelfish
Scientific Name *Centropyge multifasciatus* (Smith and Radcliffe), 1911
Habitat Coral reef, rocky reef
Distribution Qld.
Depth Range 20 to 35 metres
Adult Size 15 centimetres
Food Habit Omnivorous: encrusting organisms
Use Aquarium fish
Occurrence Rare

Living around the fissures and undercuts of steep cliff faces and reef drop-offs at the northern end of the Great Barrier Reef, it is not surprising that this little fish has been seen by very few divers. In many ways it resembles a butterflyfish, or coralfish, more than it does an angelfish. This is due to its rather deep body and its habit of raising its dorsal spines. Dwelling in fairly deep water, *C. multifasciatus* is difficult to find and get close to, especially with so many cracks and crevices to hide in beneath ledges and caves.

Multi-barred angelfish *(C. multifasciatus)*

Family POMACANTHIDAE
Common Name Bicolor angelfish
Scientific Name *Centropyge bicolor* (Bloch), 1787
Habitat Coral reef, rocky reef
Distribution Qld. (also NSW)
Depth Range 1 to 10 metres
Adult Size 15 centimetres
Food Habit Omnivorous: encrusting organisms, algae
Use Aquarium fish
Occurrence Common

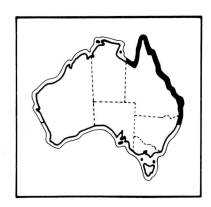

If *C. bicolor* was as bold as it was beautiful, it would be much less difficult to photograph. The bicolor angelfish inhabits areas of reef and broken bottom in lagoons, and on the slopes of back reefs in sheltered shallow water, remaining within a defined territory, sometimes shared by several adults and juveniles. More open ranging than *C. bispinosus*, *C. bicolor* swims very rapidly when moving from one coral patch to another. This species occurs throughout the Great Barrier Reef and occupies fringing reef around continental islands. It is fairly easy to maintain in an aquarium.

Bicolor angelfish *(C. bicolor)*

Family POMACANTHIDAE
Common Name Black-spot angelfish
Scientific Name *Genicanthus melanospilus* Bleeker, 1857
Habitat Coral reef
Distribution Qld.
Depth Range 20 to 30 metres
Adult Size 18 centimetres
Food Habit Carnivorous: zooplankton
Use Aquarium fish
Occurrence Rare

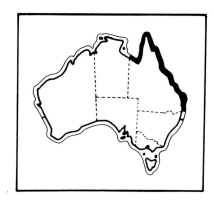

This small, elusive, unusual species lives in deeper waters on reef slopes and at the bottom of reef drop-offs where the male occupies a territory around some high point on the bottom. As in other species of this genus, the males and females are remarkably different in colour pattern and form, so much so that in some cases males and females have been described as two separate species. Unlike *G. semicinctus* (*Australian Sea Fishes South 30°S*), the male *G. melanospilus* has only one or two females in his territory and these do not form groups as do the females of *G. semicinctus*. The black-spot angelfish inhabits the northern outer areas of the Great Barrier Reef.

Black-spot angelfish *(G. melanospilus)*, female. Inset: male

Family POMACANTHIDAE
Common Name Regal angelfish
Scientific Name *Pygoplites diacanthus* (Boddaert), 1772
Habitat Coral reef, rocky reef
Distribution Qld., NT, WA
Depth Range 10 to 25 metres
Adult Size 22 centimetres
Food Habit Carnivorous: encrusting sessile organisms
Use Aquarium fish
Occurrence Common

The regal angelfish is a common species on the Great Barrier Reef and in the Coral Sea. This fish is exceptionally beautiful and is a favourite of underwater photographers. Found on reef slopes adjacent to channels, on reef drop-offs, and in the deeper parts of some lagoons, *P. diacanthus* feeds during the day and has been observed biting pieces from encrusting sessile organisms attached to cave walls and underhangs. Although they are known to pair, most of the ones I have seen have been solitary. As do many of the larger angelfish, they swim constantly and are territorial. This species requires a large tank.

Regal angelfish *(P. diacanthus)*

Family POMACENTRIDAE
Common Name Golden damsel
Scientific Name *Amblyglyphidodon aureus* (Cuvier), 1830
Habitat Coral reef
Distribution Qld., NT
Depth Range 10 to 20 metres
Adult Size 10 centimetres
Food Habit Ominvorous: zooplankton, algae
Use Aquarium fish
Occurrence Moderately common

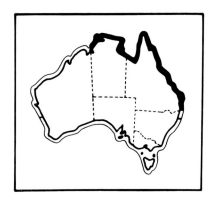

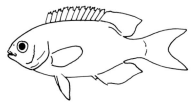

Golden damsels prefer a deeper habitat than many other damsels and are usually found several metres down the fronts of cliff faces, or drop-offs on front and back reefs. They are also seen on the edges and pinnacles of bommies and coral heads. In every case they seem to select a territory with some high object in it, either a sea fan, soft coral, black coral, or a small coral outcrop. During the day they remain around or above this object swimming up high then racing down in the typical damsel fashion. *A. aureus* is a solitary fish and is reasonably easy to get close to. In the ultra-blue water of the northern Great Barrier Reef, this fish is stunning.

Golden damsel *(A. aureus)*

Family POMACENTRIDAE
Common Name Staghorn damsel
Scientific Name *Amblyglyphidodon curacao* (Bloch), 1787
Habitat Coral reef
Distribution Qld., WA
Depth Range 3 to 15 metres
Adult Size 9 centimetres
Food Habit Ominvorous: zooplankton, crustaceans, algae
Use Aquarium fish
Occurrence Common

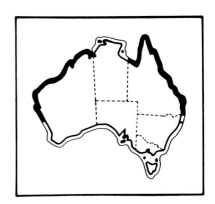

Large groups of this little damsel shelter amongst the spike-like branches of staghorn coral in calm areas of lagoons, or along the edges of reef slopes and back reef drop-offs; they may also live beneath ledges formed by other living corals where they may be seen singularly. They are quite a cheeky fish and easily approached underwater. Colour varies somewhat over their distribution, with those found on the southern Great Barrier Reef having greeny-grey backs, white undersides and with four darker green bands down the body.

Staghorn damsel *(A. curacao)*

Family POMACENTRIDAE
Common Name Blue demoiselle
Scientific Name *Glyphidodontops cyaneus* (Quoy and Gaimard), 1824
Habitat Coral reef, rocky reef
Distribution Qld., NT (also NSW)
Depth Range 5 to 20 metres
Adult Size 7 centimetres
Food Habit omnivorous
Use Aquarium fish
Occurrence Common

Commonly encountered on tropical coral reefs, blue demoiselles live in the shallow protected areas of lagoons, back reefs and/or bommies, in the proximity of lush coral growths. They generally occupy a territory adjacent to several other intraspecific territories. This species is subject to some variation throughout its distribution and may be uniform blue or with various patches of gold, discernible on the lower part of the body. Underwater, the fish shows little or no regard for a diver and most can be photographed without difficulty. Juveniles often swim in small groups. They make excellent aquarium pets.

Blue demoiselle *(G. cyaneus)*

Family POMACENTRIDAE
Common Name Southern damsel
Scientific Name *Glyphidodontops notialis* Allen, 1975
Habitat Rocky reef, coral reef
Distribution Qld. (also NSW)
Depth Range 3 to 40 metres
Adult Size 11 centimetres
Food Habit Ominvorous: crustaceans, zooplankton
Use Aquarium fish
Occurrence Common

The southern damsel occupies a number of habitats and may be seen hovering above lush tropical reef, scooting around rocky reef outcrops, or maintaining a territory on some isolated little coral clump out in the middle of a continental island sandspit. In some locations at least, the southern damsel is a diurnal planktivore selecting items from the water column during early morning and late afternoon.

Southern damsel *(G. notialis)*

Family POMACENTRIDAE
Common Name Clown anemonefish
Scientific Name *Amphiprion ocellaris* Cuvier, 1830
Habitat Coral reef
Distribution Qld., NT, WA
Depth Range 2 to 20 metres
Adult Size 7 centimetres
Food Habit Omnivorous: algae, zooplankton
Use Aquarium fish
Occurrence Common

This fish is popular in aquariums and is probably everyone's idea of a typical anemonefish. They usually live in large sea anemones such as *Radianthus ritteri* and *Stoichactis giganteum*, although specimens can be maintained in aquaria without their anemone hosts. *A. ocellaris* is found on inshore reefs and offshore reefs. Around the Darwin area, the bright orange colouration sometimes takes on a black shade. There is normally a pair of adult fish and several juveniles occupying the same anemone.

Clown anemonefish *(A. ocellaris)*

Family POMACENTRIDAE
Common Name Pink anemonefish
Scientific Name *Amphiprion perideraion* Bleeker, 1855
Habitat Coral reef, rocky reef
Distribution Qld., NT, WA
Depth Range 3 to 20 metres
Adult Size 7 centimetres
Food Habit Omnivorous: zooplankton, algae
Use Aquarium fish
Occurrence Moderately common

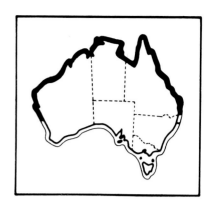

One of the most attractive and easily identified anemonefish, this species inhabits large sea anemones. Its most common host is the giant *Radianthus ritteri* which is generally found in depths below five metres where it is attached to the reef with an adhesive foot. Each time I have encountered this anemonefish there have been two adults and up to five juvenile fishes living amongst the anemone's tentacles. In north Western Australia they live in 20 metres of water at the base of exposed reef fronts in rather turbulent conditions. These fish breed in summer, with the female laying eggs on the substrate beneath the side of the anemone.

Pink anemonefish *(A. perideraion)*

Family POMACENTRIDAE
Common Name Black anemonefish
Scientific Name *Amphiprion melanopus* Bleeker, 1852
Habitat Coral reef
Distribution Qld.
Depth Range 3 to 10 metres
Adult Size 8 centimetres
Food Habit Omnivorous: algae, crustaceans
Use Aquarium fish
Occurrence Moderately common

Not all anemonefish live in large sea anemones — some live in colonies of smaller sea anemones, which when expanded give the impression of one large one. The black anemonefish is an associate of *Physobrachia douglasi* which often dwell around the bases of coral clumps. Sometimes when disturbed, the sea anemone contracts and leaves the little anemonefish to seek shelter in the coral. This has led to reports of anemonefish without a host anemone.

Black anemonefish *(A. melanopus)*

Family POMACENTRIDAE
Common Name Jewel damsel
Scientific Name *Plectroglyphidodon lacrymatus* (Quoy and Gaimard), 1825
Habitat Coral reef
Distribution Qld., WA (also NSW)
Depth Range 4 to 12 metres
Adult Size 8 centimetres
Food Habit Omnivorous: algae
Use Aquarium fish
Occurrence Common

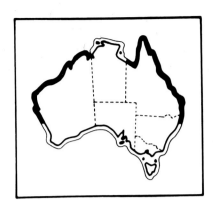

Jewel damsels are found on the Great Barrier Reef in areas of sheltered lagoons and back reef, as well as around continental island and mainland reefs. They are generally seen alone in areas of sheltered water, where they maintain a territory that has at least one escape hole. During the day, individuals patrol their territory, guarding against other herbivorous fishes whilst feeding. Single specimens are quite hardy in home aquaria.

Jewel damsel *(P. lacrymatus)*

Family POMACENTRIDAE
Common Name Reticulated dascyllus
Scientific Name *Dascyllus reticulatus* (Richardson), 1846
Habitat Coral reef
Distribution Qld., NT, WA (also NSW)
Depth Range 1 to 20 metres
Adult Size 6 centimetres
Food Habit Omnivorous: zooplankton
Use Aquarium fish
Occurrence Common

The reticulated dascyllus is a small, easily identified pomacentrid which inhabits lagoons and back reefs and generally occurs in shallow waters. It doesn't vary much in colour, and is often seen in the company of *Dascyllus aruanus*. The habitat of *D. reticulatus* is in, or around, isolated patch reefs of staghorn corals on sandy bottom, reef slopes or growing adjacent to larger patches of reef. Although some specimens may be seen solitarily, most live in groups, where they use the staghorn coral as a fortress, rising above to feed in the water and quickly taking cover when threatened.

Reticulated dascyllus *(D. reticulatus)*

Family POMACENTRIDAE
Common Name Blue-green chromis
Scientific Name *Chromis caerulea* (Cuvier), 1830
Habitat Rocky reef, coral reef
Distribution Qld., NT, WA (also NSW)
Depth Range 1 to 12 metres
Adult Size 6 centimetres
Food Habit Omnivorous: zooplankton
Use Aquarium fish
Occurrence Very common

The experience of watching hundreds of these emerald fish swim out of their coral abodes and rise up with the sun at daybreak in a mass underwater ballet is unforgettable. The colour of *C. caerulea* is somewhat variable and ranges from iridescent green, to iridescent blue. Their habitat is largely staghorn corals in sheltered lagoons and along the edges and terraces of back reefs.

Blue-green chromis *(C. caerulea)*

Family CIRRHITIDAE
Common Name Spotted hawkfish
Scientific Name *Cirrhitichthys oxycephalus* (Bleeker), 1855
Habitat Coral reef, rocky reef
Distribution Qld.
Depth Range 10 to 25 metres
Adult Size 8 centimetres
Food Habit Carnivorous: crustaceans
Use Aquarium fish
Occurrence Uncommon

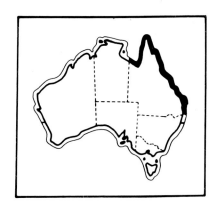

The spotted hawkfish is one of the smaller hawkfishes inhabiting the fringing reefs of the northern extremities of the Great Barrier Reef. Due to its size and its habit of utilizing the lower areas of the reef amongst coral, *C. oxycephalus* escapes the notice of most divers. When in the undergrowth, the spotted hawkfish tends to select places of medium height on which to sit on the lookout for prey.

Spotted hawkfish *(C. oxycephalus)*

Family CIRRHITIDAE
Common Name Ring-eyed hawkfish
Scientific Name *Paracirrhites arcatus* (Cuvier), 1829
Habitat Coral reef
Distribution Qld., WA
Depth Range 2 to 20 metres
Adult Size 15 centimetres
Food Habit Carnivorous: crustaceans, fish
Use Aquarium fish
Occurrence Common

Quite common and easily approached underwater, the ring-eyed hawk-fish is an attractive fish found from the centre of the Great Barrier Reef, northwards around fringing continental island reefs and out into the Coral Sea. It is probably the most conspicuous of all the hawkfish for it sits on the tops of coral and hydro-corals out in the open swooping down on small prey. It is possible that *P. arcatus* also feeds directly from the water around it.

Ring-eyed hawkfish *(P. arcatus)*

Family CIRRHITIDAE
Common Name Forster's hawkfish
Scientific Name *Paracirrhites forsteri* (Bloch and Schneider), 1801
Habitat Coral reef
Distribution Qld., WA
Depth Range 2 to 10 metres
Adult Size 25 centimetres
Food Habit Carnivorous: crustaceans
Use Aquarium fish
Occurrence Common

One of the largest of the tropical hawkfishes, *P. forsteri* has several different colour phases, including a black one. Forster's hawkfish lives around fringing reefs of northern continental islands on the northern Great Barrier Reef, and in the Coral Sea. During the day it sits amongst the branches of staghorn corals *(Acropora)* where it also sleeps at night. *P. forsteri* is a territorial fish that is easily approached by divers.

Forster's hawkfish *(P. forsteri)*

Family CIRRHITIDAE
Common Name Long-nosed hawkfish
Scientific Name *Oxycirrhites typus* Bleeker, 1857
Habitat Coral reef
Distribution Qld.
Depth Range 20 to 30 metres
Adult Size 14 centimetres
Food Habit Carnivorous: crustaceans
Use Aquarium
Occurrence Rare

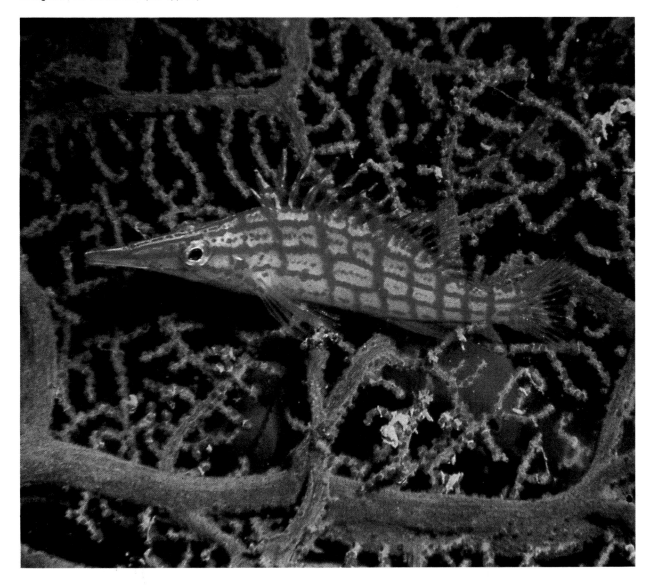

This fish is another example where underwater photography has established the presence of a fish in Australian waters before it has been collected. Roger Steene was the first person to record this species on the northern Great Barrier Reef; it is also known to occur in the Coral Sea.

A beautiful and unique species, this territorial hawkfish lives amongst the branches of black coral trees and giant sea fans that are attached to cliff faces and drop-offs. Very often there is a pair of fish on one sea fan and it is assumed that they are male and female. Easily approached underwater *O. typus* makes an ideal aquarium fish.

Long-nosed hawkfish *(O. typus)*

Family MUGILIDAE
Common Name Sea mullet
Scientific Name *Mugil cephalus* Linnaeus, 1758
Habitat Estuaries, open ocean
Distribution Qld., WA, NT (also NSW)
Depth Range Surface to 20 metres
Adult Size 76 centimetres
Food Habit Omnivorous: algae, detritus, crustaceans
Use Edible
Occurrence Common

Sea mullet are found in coastal waters, though stragglers do make their way out to the Great Barrier Reef. Young fish spend their lives in the estuaries and enter fresh water. These fish migrate north annually to spawn and during this migration are netted commercially. After spawning, large adults may penetrate well into estuaries where they are captured by a variety of methods — they are shot, speared, tagged, as well as being caught by line, rod and net. Some estuarine specimens are prone to lesions. A popular food fish, sea mullet are at their best when grilled over an open fire.

Sea mullet *(M. cephalus)*

Family LABRIDAE
Common Name Black-spot tuskfish
Scientific Name *Choerodon schoenleinii* (Cuvier and Valenciennes), 1839
Habitat Coral reef, rocky reef
Distribution Qld., WA, NT
Depth Range 4 to 30 metres
Adult Size 1 metre
Food Habit Carnivorous: molluscs, crustaceans
Use Edible
Occurrence Common

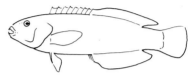

The black-spot tuskfish is a large fish found in lagoons and the deeper waters along the terraces and fringes of back reefs throughout the Great Barrier Reef. During the day it can be seen foraging amongst dead coral rubble and around the edges of coral slabs lying on sand. This fish uses its large tusk-like teeth to pick up and turn over quite enormous pieces of coral and shingle. It drags these to one side, then lays down on its side in the hole and fans the sand away with its pectoral fins, exposing molluscs and crabs which are immediately seized and swallowed. This species readily accepts cut fish baits and is itself very good eating.

Black-spot tuskfish *(C. schoenleinii)*

Family LABRIDAE
Common Name Graphic tuskfish
Scientific Name *Choerodon graphicus* (De Vis), 1885
Habitat Coral reef
Distribution Qld.
Depth Range 5 to 30 metres
Adult Size 45 centimetres
Food Habit Carnivorous: molluscs, crustaceans
Use Edible
Occurrence Common

Easily recognised and approached underwater, the graphic tuskfish is a very adept hunter and employs a number of different tactics to obtain its prey. On coral rubble, the graphic tuskfish will dig a hole by removing pieces bit by bit with its teeth and placing them aside. It then gets in the hole and, by vigorous fanning with fins and tail, stirs up the bottom in a flurry of coral dust. It will then back off and watch for any movement. If not successful, it repeats the process until it finds what it has somehow sensed. This species occurs throughout the Great Barrier Reef, can be caught by line and has firm white flesh.

Graphic tuskfish *(C. graphicus)*

Family LABRIDAE
Common Name Blue tuskfish
Scientific Name *Choerodon albigena* (De Vis), 1885
Habitat Coral reef, rocky reef
Distribution Qld., NT
Depth Range 1 to 25 metres
Adult Size 71 centimetres
Food Habit Carnivorous: molluscs
Use Edible
Occurrence Common

A good sized food fish normally feeding on molluscs, the blue tuskfish is easily caught with handlines, or cut fish baits. *C. albigena* tends to enter very shallow waters on top of the reef flats and during low water is often caught in tide pools. Some specimens have been found in just a few centimetres of water lying on their sides beneath dead coral slabs where they have taken shelter to wait for the returning tide. *C. albigena* is regularly speared in Queensland waters, for it lives on coastal reefs and continental islands, as well as throughout the Great Barrier Reef. When cleared, it has green or bluish bones, but this should not deter anybody from eating the flesh as it is very succulent.

Blue tuskfish *(C. albigena)*

Family LABRIDAE
Common Name Harlequin tuskfish
Scientific Name *Choerodon fasciatus* (Günther), 1867
Habitat Coral reef
Distribution Qld.
Depth Range 5 to 30 metres
Adult Size 30 centimetres
Food Habit Carnivorous: molluscs, crustaceans, worms, echinoderms
Use Aquarium fish
Occurrence Common

The harlequin tuskfish is a territorial species which occurs along the Great Barrier Reef into the Coral Sea. With such a colour pattern there is no mistaking this fish and due to its boldness it is not difficult to get close to underwater. *C. fasciatus* soon learns that divers inadvertently provide access to food by stirring up the bottom and dislodging small creatures and it will often swim close by, sometimes becoming a nuisance. The males and females (unlike most other tuskfish) are difficult to tell apart in the field.

Harlequin tuskfish *(C. fasciatus)*

Family LABRIDAE
Common Name Scarlet-breasted maori wrasse
Scientific Name *Cheilinus fasciatus* (Bloch), 1791
Habitat Coral reef
Distribution Qld., NT, WA
Depth Range 8 to 25 metres
Adult Size 35 centimetres
Food Habit Carnivorous: molluscs
Use Edible
Occurrence Common

Rarely encountered in southern areas, this species is common on the fringing reefs of continental islands and along the northern areas of the Great Barrier Reef. *C. fasciatus* inhabits reef slopes and terraces adjacent to channels and also lives in lagoons below the reef edge. It is a diurnal hunter which occupies a territory having at least two hiding places into which it can retreat. The scarlet-breasted maori wrasse is a slow swimming fish which browses around and generally picks up its food from the underside of ledges, small caves and crevices in the reef.

Scarlet-breasted maori wrasse *(C. fasciatus)*

Family LABRIDAE
Common Name Violet-lined maori wrasse
Scientific Name *Cheilinus diagrammus* (Lacépède), 1802
Habitat Coral reef, rocky reef
Distribution Qld., NT, WA
Depth Range 2 to 25 metres
Adult Size 38 centimetres
Food Habit Carnivorous: crustaceans, molluscs
Use Aquarium fish
Occurrence Common

Found throughout the entire Great Barrier Reef system, *C. Diagrammus* can also be seen around the fringing reefs of continental islands and some mainland reefs. Similar to *C. fasciatus*, this species hovers, using hard corals, soft corals and sea fans as camouflage while hunting. C. diagrammus is easy to get close to underwater and during the night sleeps deep in coral grottoes. Unlike some wrasse it does not go to sleep at sunset and individuals may still be seen in midwater, or in caves, as late as 8 pm.

Violet-lined maori wrasse *(C. diagrammus)*

Family LABRIDAE
Common Name Giant maori wrasse
Scientific Name *Cheilinus undulatus* Rüppell, 1835
Habitat Coral reef
Distribution Qld., NT, WA
Depth Range 10 to 40 metres
Adult Size 2.3 metres
Food Habit Carnivorous: molluscs, crustaceans
Use Edible
Occurrence Moderately common

A veritable giant of a fish and by far the largest wrasse, the giant maori wrasse is mostly seen along the deeper parts of reef fronts that have sandy, rubble terraces, where deep gaps lead into the reef, along the slopes of channels and deeper places in lagoons. Very often, several fish may swim together headstanding amongst the dead coral and rubble to tear up the bottom in their search for molluscs and crabs. Although large samples have been caught by line, these fish are more susceptible to spearfishing, for when chased they hole up and very often can be speared within their retreats. Medium sized fish make good eating, but large ones are somewhat tough.

Giant maori wrasse *(C. undulatus)*

213

Family LABRIDAE
Common Name Triple-tail maori wrasse
Scientific Name *Cheilinus trilobatus* Lacépède, 1802
Habitat Coral reef
Distribution Qld., NT, WA
Depth Range 2 to 10 metres
Adult Size 66 centimetres
Food Habit Carnivorous: crustaceans
Use Edible
Occurrence Common

The triple-tail maori wrasse is a shallow water, territorial species with the male maintaining a territory along the edges of back reefs, fringing reefs and lagoons. The territory may be marked by a high piece of coral or some other significant object and may extend over 20 square metres. Within the territory there may be up to six females, usually swimming as a group. The male continually patrols the perimeter, occasionally rounding up the females that stray too close to the edges and chasing other males, as far as 15 metres away from the territory. This species is more common in the central and northern areas of the Great Barrier Reef.

Triple-tail maori wrasse *(C. trilobatus)*, male

Family LABRIDAE
Common Name Thick-lipped wrasse
Scientific Name *Hemigymnus melapterus* (Bloch), 1791
Habitat Rocky reef, coral reef
Distribution Qld., NT, WA (also NSW)
Depth Range 3 to 25 metres
Adult Size 1 metre
Food Habit Carnivorous: molluscs, crustaceans, worms
Use Edible
Occurrence Common

The thick-lipped wrasse is more familiar to snorkellers, divers and spearfishermen than it is to line fishermen, for due to its diet and feeding behaviour few are caught on hand lines. This species lives along the length of the Great Barrier Reef where it generally inhabits lagoons and during the day swims around areas of broken bottom and sandy rubble. When feeding, the thick-lipped wrasse sucks in a mouthful of detritus from the bottom, sorts out the edible portion inside the mouth, swallows the food and allows the residue to trickle out through the gill covers. It is fairly easy to approach underwater and is good eating.

Thick-lipped wrasse *(H. melapterus)*

Family LABRIDAE
Common Name Bird wrasse
Scientific Name *Gomphosus varius* Lacépède, 1802
Habitat Coral reef
Distribution Qld., NT, WA (also NSW)
Depth Range 5 to 20 metres
Adult Size 25 centimetres
Food Habit Carnivorous: crustaceans
Use Aquarium fish
Occurrence Common

The bird wrasse is easily identified by the large protruding 'beak'. A swimming behaviour of sculling with its pectorals in typical wrasse-like fashion, give it an even more bird-like image as it flits around in shallow coral areas of the Great Barrier Reef. Female bird wrasses are much more commonly encountered and several may be seen swimming together. This species will also swim with groups of other wrasses as they feed. The male is a similar shape to the female; though larger, it has a blue beak and head with a yellow-green blotch above the pectoral fins. The central part of the body is green, blending into a blue caudal peduncle and tail.

Bird wrasse *(G. varius)*, female

Family LABRIDAE
Common Name Painted rainbow wrasse
Scientific Name *Suezichthys* sp (Labrid N°90 A.M.P.I.)
Habitat Coral reef, rocky reef
Distribution Qld. (also NSW)
Depth Range 15 to 30 metres
Adult Size 15 centimetres
Food Habit Carnivorous: crustaceans
Use Aquarium fish
Occurrence Uncommon

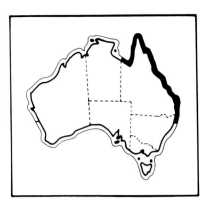

A very attractive, yet undescribed wrasse which inhabits the deeper waters out from reef edges on sand rubble and broken bottom is the painted rainbow wrasse, *Suezichthys* sp. Even though there are close to 3000 marine fishes recorded from Australian waters new species are being found almost daily. It may be years before these descriptions are published. This fish was recently sighted at the Admiralty Islands off Lord Howe Island and is a new record for that area. Only one family group was sighted, including a male, female and juvenile. The male is exceedingly shy underwater and difficult to get close to.

Painted rainbow wrasse *(Suezichthys* sp), female

Family LABRIDAE
Common Name Sling-jaw wrasse
Scientific Name *Epibulus insidiator* (Pallas), 1770
Habitat Coral reef
Distribution Qld., NT, WA (also NSW)
Depth Range 3 to 25 metres
Adult Size 33 centimetres
Food Habit Carnivorous: crustaceans
Use Edible
Occurrence Moderately common

While the male *E. insidiator* is quite conspicuous amongst the coral gardens of the Great Barrier Reef, the female, due to her drab colouration, is generally overlooked. This species has unique extendible jaws which can telescope out and catch prey in a flash. The sling-jaw wrasse is territorial, though I have never seen more than one female at a time within the male's territory. *E. insidiator* prefers rich coral cover in shallow water, and may be seen in sheltered lagoons, or on reef fronts. It is a rather timid fish.

Sling-jaw wrasse *(E. insidiator)*, male. Inset: female

Family LABRIDAE
Common Name Axil pigfish
Scientific Name *Bodianus axillaris* (Bennett), 1831
Habitat Coral reefs
Distribution Qld., WA (also NSW)
Depth Range 2 to 20 metres
Adult Size 20 centimetres
Food Habit Carnivorous: crustaceans
Use Aquarium fish
Occurrence Common

The axil pigfish is often sighted throughout the entire Great Barrier Reef system and although it is reasonably simple to get close to underwater, its contrasting colouration makes photography difficult.

B. axillaris is territorial and may be observed to swim in set patterns in and around that territory; the patterns may often be repetitive. The juveniles are totally dissimilar in colour and pattern to the adults and in the middle 1960s were thought to be a new species. Whereas adults may be seen out in the open, flitting around ledges and over reefs close to the bottom, the juveniles are found in caves.

The juvenile makes an excellent aquarium fish.

Axil pigfish *(B. axillaris)*, juvenile.   Inset: adult

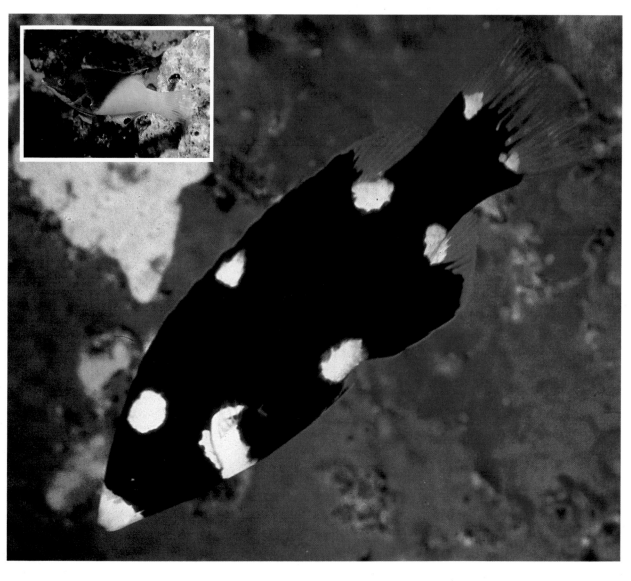

Family LABRIDAE
Common Name Reef pigfish
Scientific Name *Bodianus loxozonus* (Snyder), 1904
Habitat Coral reef
Distribution Qld.
Depth Range 3 to 40 metres
Adult Size 40 centimetres
Food Habit Carnivorous: molluscs, crustaceans
Use Edible
Occurrence Uncommon

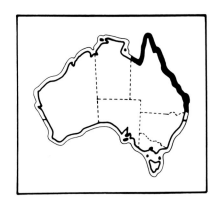

A resident of the more northern parts of the Great Barrier Reef, *B. loxozonus* is a spectacular species which inhabits both shallow lagoons and the deep waters of reef front drop-offs. It is territorial, and shallow water males may have several females within a territory. Not always easy to approach underwater, they seem far less shy on the Great Barrier Reef than they do in the Coral Sea. As yet I haven't seen these fish on night dives and this may be due to their habit of sleeping beneath the sand as do other members of their genus. Rarely caught on hand lines.

Reef pigfish *(B. loxozonus)*

Family LABRIDAE
Common Name Diana's pigfish
Scientific Name *Bodianus diana* (Lacépède), 1802
Habitat Coral reef
Distribution Qld. (also NSW)
Depth Range 10 to 30 metres
Adult Size 25 centimetres
Food Habit Carnivorous: crustaceans
Use Aquarium fish
Occurrence Uncommon

Unlike many other pigfishes that are commonly seen out in the open reef and amongst the lagoonal coral growths, Diana's pigfish is a rather shy, secretive species which lives on cliff faces and drop-offs in deeper waters. During the day it can be seen swimming up and down the reef faces on front, or back reefs, searching the ledges, caves, gutters and crevices for food. This fish is found throughout the entire Great Barrier Reef, but is far more prolific in the northern areas. Similar to the adults, the juveniles of *B. diana* are also territorial and may be found living in caves.

Diana's pigfish *(B. diana)*

Family LABRIDAE
Common Name Banda wrasse
Scientific Name *Stethojulius bandanensis* (Bleeker), 1851
Habitat Coral reef
Distribution Qld., NT, WA (also NSW)
Depth Range 1 to 10 metres
Adult Size 12 centimetres
Food Habit Carnivorous: crustaceans
Use Aquarium fish
Occurrence Moderately common

A small, very fast swimming wrasse, both the male and female of *S. bandanensis* are attractive. The rather incredible example of sexual dichromatism in this species has led many people including ichthyologists to regard them as separate species. The banda wrasse is primarily a shallow water fish which inhabits rich coral areas, or reef tops and slopes, in lagoons. The males are territorial and at times may have small groups of females (up to four or five fish) within his territory.

Banda wrasse *(S. bandanensis)*, female. Inset: male

Family LABRIDAE
Common Name Moon wrasse
Scientific Name *Thalassoma lunare* (Linnaeus), 1758
Habitat Rocky reef, coral reef
Distribution Qld., NT, WA (also NSW)
Depth Range 1 to 20 metres
Adult Size 30 centimetres
Food Habit Carnivorous: molluscs, crustaceans
Use Aquarium fish
Occurrence Common

The gaudy male moon wrasse is one of the most numerous wrasses on the reef, flitting along above the corals. Females can be distinguished from the males by the absence of the crescent shaped blue tail with its yellow centre. The tail of the female is generally transparent with a hint of blue and red at the leading edges. Younger ones have a black blotch on the caudal peduncle and a small black spot halfway along the soft dorsal. The female also lacks the strongly coloured pectoral of the male. This species generally inhabits sheltered lagoons and back reef areas and often swims in groups.

Moon wrasse *(T. lunare)*, male

Family LABRIDAE
Common Name Blue-head wrasse
Scientific Name *Thalassoma amblycephala* (Bleeker), 1856
Habitat Rocky reef, coral reef
Distribution Qld., WA (also NSW)
Depth Range 1 to 10 metres
Adult Size 15 centimetres
Food Habit Carnivorous: crustaceans
Use Aquarium fish
Occurrence Common

Although the blue-head wrasse is found throughout the Great Barrier Reef and on some of the continental islands, it seems to be localised. It lives in shallow water in lagoons and prefers protected reefs, where it spends a great deal of its time swimming one to two metres above the reef. This fish is a very fast moving wrasse and although it can be readily approached, *T. amblycephala* is always a challenge to photograph. Females swim in groups of up to 15 and are dark blue on the top half of the body with dozens of thin black bands on upper sides. The lower half of the body is white.

Blue-head wrasse *(T. amblycephala)*, male

Family LABRIDAE
Common Name Japanese rainbow wrasse
Scientific Name *Cirrhilabrus temmincki* Bleeker, 1852
Habitat Coral reef
Distribution Qld., WA (also NSW)
Depth Range 1 to 20 metres
Adult Size 20 centimetres
Food Habit Carnivorous: crustaceans
Use Aquarium fish
Occurrence Common

A delightful little wrasse frequenting lagoons and sheltered back reefs as well as terraces and slopes of reef fronts, *C. temmincki* is found throughout the Great Barrier Reef. It is absent from some reefs, while at others it is most abundant. The Japanese rainbow wrasse spends a lot of time about two metres off the bottom. The females swim in a group and several males may swim around and through the group displaying their colourful dorsal and ventral fins. This genus is recognised by the exceptionally long pelvic fins which are lowered when the male displays.

Japanese rainbow wrasse *(C. temmincki)*, male

Family LABRIDAE
Common Name Olive-scribbled wrasse
Scientific Name *Xyrichtys taeniouris* (Lacépède), 1802
Habitat Coral reef
Distribution Qld., NT, WA (also NSW)
Depth Range 2 to 15 metres
Adult Size 30 centimetres
Food Habit Carnivorous: crustaceans
Use Aquarium fish
Occurrence Uncommon

The young juveniles of *X. taeniouris* are absolutely exquisite, being beautifully marked and with such a long head adornment it might be expected that these fishes would be easy to see. Strangely enough this is not so underwater, as they swim in a very peculiar manner close to the bottom and sometimes on their sides. When they are side swimming they alternate from side to side to look remarkably like a piece of loose bottom debris, being wafted to and fro by the water. The adults are easily identified and generally swim together in pairs and sometimes in threes, or fours. They are very determined in searching for food and stir up clouds of silt, particularly on coral rubble bottom.

Olive-scribbled wrasse *(X. taeniouris)*, juvenile. Inset: adult

Family LABRIDAE
Common Name Dotted wrasse
Scientific Name *Anampses meleagrides* Cuvier and Valenciennes, 1839
Habitat Coral reef
Distribution Qld., NT, WA (also NSW)
Depth Range 2 to 20 metres
Adult Size 20 centimetres
Food Habit Carnivorous: crustaceans
Use Aquarium fish
Occurrence Uncommon

There is often a lot of time involved between sighting a species of fish and getting a good photograph. I recognised this species five years before I got a reasonable photo. The dotted wrasse is a fast swimming elusive species which lives in the northern reaches of the Great Barrier Reef and can be seen in sheltered lagoons and backreef areas, as well as along the terraces of reef fronts and slopes where there is open, broken coral bottom. It should make an excellent aquarium fish.

Dotted wrasse *(A. meleagrides)*, female

Family LABRIDAE
Common Name South seas wrasse
Scientific Name *Anampses femininus* Randall, 1972
Habitat Coral reef, rocky reef
Distribution Qld., WA (also NSW)
Depth Range 10 to 30 metres
Adult Size 20 centimetres
Food Habit Carnivorous: crustaceans
Use Aquarium fish
Occurrence Uncommon

There are many small exquisite wrasse — the males in particular are gaudy, as if painted to extravagance. In other cases the very small juveniles may be the most colourful. I think the south seas female is without doubt one of the most beautiful of fish. Young females often swim in groups of three or four and tend to be territorial. *A. femininus* does not seem to be common in any one area and has been recorded from mainland and offshore islands and reefs.

South seas wrasse *(A. femininus)*, female

Family LABRIDAE
Common Name Elegant wrasse
Scientific Name *Anampses elegans* Ogilby, 1889
Habitat Coral reef, rocky reef
Distribution Qld. (also NSW)
Depth Range 2 to 35 metres
Adult Size 30 centimetres
Food Habit Carnivorous: crustaceans, molluscs
Use Aquarium fish
Occurrence Common

Although the male elegant wrasse seems to be territorial in shallow waters, in deeper areas it may range over several hundred metres during feeding forays. The females often form huge schools and I have seen one such school of 80 to 100 individual adult females foraging at 28 metres at Lord Howe Island. Females are basically the same size as the male, greenish-yellow on the top half and white on the bottom half with a yellow tail and ventral fin. Females are without the bright blues of the male and lack the bright yellow blotches on the back of the gill plates, though they do have a yellow mark at the base of the pectoral fin.

Elegant wrasse *(A. elegans)*, male

Family LABRIDAE
Common Name Bicolor cleaner wrasse
Scientific Name *Labroides bicolor* Fowler and Bean, 1928
Habitat Coral reef
Distribution Qld., NT, WA (also NSW)
Depth Range 1 to 20 metres
Adult Size 12 centimetres
Food Habit Carnivorous: crustaceans
Use Aquarium fish
Occurrence Moderately common

Certainly nowhere near as common as *L. dimidiatus,* the bicolor cleaner wrasse inhabits coral areas along the entire Great Barrier Reef and in the Coral Sea. This species may be observed in lagoons in the vicinity of back reefs and also on terraces and in deeper surge channels on some reef fronts. *L. bicolor* may be seen in pairs, or alone. Other cleaner wrasses have fairly definite and often fairly small territorial cleaning stations where other fish come to be cleaned. The bicolor cleaner wrasse is territorial, but is more widely ranging in its search for host fishes and far more aggressive in its approach, often chasing the host high above the bottom.

Bicolor cleaner wrasse *(L. bicolor)*

Family SCARIDAE
Common Name Green and blue parrotfish
Scientific Name *Scarus frenatus* (Lacépède), 1802
Habitat Coral reef
Distribution Qld., WA (also NSW)
Depth Range 5 to 20 metres
Adult Size 35 centimetres
Food Habit Herbivorous: algae
Use Edible
Occurrence Common

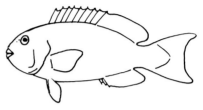

Similar to the wrasses, the sexual dichromatism within the family Scaridae has led to a great deal of taxonomic confusion. This problem, coupled with the marked differences in many juveniles, has made parrotfishes one of the most difficult families to identify underwater. *S. frenatus* occurs along the entire Great Barrier Reef and the Coral Sea. Green and blue parrotfish are not easily approached underwater, few are caught on lines, though they are quite good eating.

Green and blue parrotfish *(S. frenatus)*, female

Family SCARIDAE
Common Name Dusky parrotfish
Scientific Name *Scarus niger* (Forsskål), 1775
Habitat Coral reef
Distribution Qld.
Depth Range 2 to 25 metres
Adult Size 40 centimetres
Food Habit Herbivorous: algae
Use Edible
Occurrence Common

This species is probably the most simple of all the parrotfishes to identify, as it varies little in colour throughout its distribution. The tail colours and the black edged green spot behind the eye are characteristic. The dusky parrotfish is generally a solitary fish, though the females are apt to forage together as a small group. These fishes feed on algae by scraping and biting live and dead coral with their fused parrot-like scalloped teeth. *S. niger* is found throughout the Great Barrier Reef in lagoons, or around sloping back reefs in sheltered water. At night it sleeps in caves in the reef.

Dusky parrotfish *(S. niger)*, male

Family SCARIDAE
Common Name Blunt-headed parrotfish
Scientific Name *Scarus gibbus* Rüppell, 1828
Habitat Coral reef
Distribution Qld., WA (also NSW)
Depth Range 2 to 30 metres
Adult Size 50 centimetres
Food Habit Herbivorous: algae
Use Edible
Occurrence Common

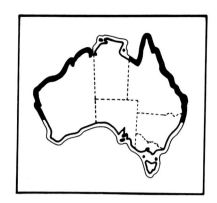

A large, easily recognised parrotfish which inhabits the slopes and terraces of back reefs, channel entrances, the bommies along the entire Great Barrier Reef. The males are usually alone, although male and female pairs are likely to be observed during summer months. At some localities this species seems to be unafraid of divers and at others it is quite shy. *S. gibbus* appears to prefer algae taken from dead coral surfaces rather than live corals though this may alter depending on location. While very few are caught on lines, numbers are taken by spearing. The flesh is of excellent quality.

Blunt-headed parrotfish *(S. gibbus)*, male

Family SCARIDAE
Common Name Green-finned parrotfish
Scientific Name *Scarus sordidus* (Forsskål), 1775
Habitat Coral reef
Distribution Qld., NT, WA (also NSW)
Depth Range 1 to 25 metres
Adult Size 45 centimetres
Food Habit Herbivorous: algae
Use Edible
Occurrence Common

The male green-finned parrotfish has greeny-blue fins, the dorsal having a single divided red or purple stripe, and the ventral having a single red or purple stripe. There is also a red stripe on the pectoral fin, towards the leading edge. Although subject to some variation throughout its range, the male almost always has an orange blush along the body beginning at the head and intensifying towards the caudal peduncle, which is light green. Females are a dull red, with red tails and a black spot at the base of the tail, on the caudal peduncle.

Green-finned parrotfish *(S. sordidus)*, male

Family SCARIDAE
Common Name Blue-barred parrotfish
Scientific Name *Scarus ghobban* Forsskål, 1775
Habitat Coral reef
Distribution Qld., NT, WA
Depth Range 1 to 30 metres
Adult Size 101 centimetres
Food Habit Herbivorous: algae
Use Edible
Occurrence Moderately common

Adult blue-barred parrotfish are generally seen in deeper water than the juveniles. They feed on algae obtained from living corals; the flesh is either scraped off coral surfaces or pieces of coral are bitten off, crunched up by pharangeal teeth in the throat and conveyed to the stomach. The organic material is digested by the fish and the coral particles are excreted as coral dust. This species may also feed on algae infesting dead coral. It is found throughout the Great Barrier Reef and is good eating.

Blue-barred parrotfish *(S. ghobban)*, male. Inset: female

Family SCARIDAE
Common Name Spiny parrotfish
Scientific Name *Scarus spinus* Kner, 1868
Habitat Coral reef
Distribution Qld.
Depth Range 3 to 15 metres
Adult Size 33 centimetres
Food Habit Herbivorous
Use Edible
Occurrence Uncommon

Parrotfish are difficult fishes to get close to underwater, as are many groups of herbivorous fishes. The spiny parrotfish is even more difficult than others. It lives in rich coral habitats in lagoons and around the slopes of back reefs along the entire Great Barrier Reef. Males are always seen alone and swim in an ill-defined territory, occasionally taking a bite of coral as they move about. *S. spinus* is one of the smaller parrotfishes but compared to other species swims very fast. The males have a fairly characteristic shape and can be distinguished by the bright yellow neckband which passes through a yellow patch above the junction of the pectoral fin.

Spiny parrotfish *(S. spinus)*, male

Family SCARIDAE
Common Name Surf parrotfish
Scientific Name *Scarus rivulatus* Valenciennes, 1839
Habitat Coral reef
Distribution Qld., NT, WA
Depth Range 1 to 20 metres
Adult Size 35 centimetres
Food Habit Herbivorous: algae
Use Edible
Occurrence Common

Parrotfish and wrasses are amongst the most beautifully adorned fishes in the sea and have confused fishermen for many years. The distinction between the two families is really quite simple as wrasses have separate teeth and parrotfishes have fused teeth. The surf parrotfish is abundant in shallow lagoons all along the Great Barrier Reef, sometimes seen coming onto the reef-flats with their backs out of the water, on the rising tide. The male has a large orange or red blotch which covers the lower portion of the gill plates. This species is good eating.

Surf parrotfish *(S. rivulatus)*, male

Family URANOSCOPIDAE
Common Name Northwest stargazer
Scientific Name *Ichthyscopus insperatus* Mees, 1960
Habitat Sand
Distribution NT, WA
Depth Range Low tide to 10 metres
Adult Size 21 centimetres
Food Habit Carnivorous
Use Edible
Occurrence Uncommon

Stargazers are an interesting group of fishes that are more familiar to professional net fishermen and trawlers than to scuba divers, snorkellers or line fishermen. This is due to their habit of burying themselves into sandy or muddy bottoms with only their eyes showing. Sometimes with a little practice it is possible to pick out their outline in the sand. Until I found a specimen off Darwin, the northwest stargazer was only recorded from the west coast. Adult specimens are darker than the one shown here, though the pattern is similar.

Northwest stargazer *(I. insperatus)*

Family BLENNIIDAE
Common Name Leopard blenny
Scientific Name *Exallias brevis* (Kner), 1868
Habitat Coral reef
Distribution Qld., WA
Depth Range 5 to 20 metres
Adult Size 9 centimetres
Food Habit Omnivorous: coral tissue and mucous
Use Aquarium fish
Occurrence Uncommon

The leopard blenny has the rather peculiar habit of sitting in clumps of coral in a semi-vertical position laying along the coral, with its head elevated. Whereas other species of blennies are seen out in the open during the day actively feeding on algae, the leopard blenny rarely leaves its coral abode. This species is one of the few blennies which is now entirely herbivorous.

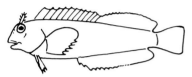

Leopard benny *(E. brevis)*

Family BLENNIIDAE
Common Name Pale-spotted coral blenny
Scientific Name *Escenius opsifrontalis* Chapman and Schultz, 1952
Habitat Coral reef
Distribution Qld.
Depth Range 8 to 20 metres
Adult Size 5 centimetres
Food Habit Omnivorous: algae
Use Aquarium fish
Occurrence Moderately common

Being small, blennies remain unseen by most divers and as they do not come up in nets and are not of sufficient size for food, very little is known about them. With well over 70 species already discovered and many new species awaiting description, blennies are one of the largest families of marine fishes. The pale-spotted coral blenny lives throughout the Great Barrier Reef and is quite commonly seen in the open, scooting about the sides of bommies and slopes, feeding on algae which it tears off with its thick lips.

Pale-spotted coral blenny *(E. opsifrontalis)*

Family BLENNIIDAE
Common Name Japanese coral blenny
Scientific Name *Escenius yaeyamaensis* (Aoyagi), 1954
Habitat Coral reef
Distribution Qld., WA
Depth Range 1 to 8 metres
Adult Size 4 centimetres
Food Habit Herbivorous: algae
Use Aquarium fish
Occurrence Uncommon

Blennies are rather comical little fish to observe, with their large heads and big eyes, they forever seem to be sitting up. When feeding, the Japanese coral blenny is similar to other algae eating blennies. It makes short sharp biting movements, cropping algae from the substrate, then sits back for a time to swallow, before repeating the process.

E. yaeyamaensis appears to be selective, and was observed to feed on filamentous algae attached to the tests of ascidians, scooting around the territory taking a few mouthfuls at a time from each ascidian. This fish occurs along the northern reaches of the Great Barrier Reef.

Japanese coral blenny *(E. yaeyamaensis)*

Family CONGROGADIDAE
Common Name Ocellated eel blenny
Scientific Name *Congrogadus subducens* (Richardson), 1843
Habitat Coral reef
Distribution Qld., NT, WA
Depth Range 1 to 5 metres
Adult Size 50 centimetres
Food Habit Carnivorous
Use Not generally eaten
Occurrence Uncommon

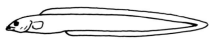

The largest of the eel blennies, *C. subducens* is a territorial carnivore that lives in lagoons in sheltered waters, and occurs on mainland and offshore reefs. With its long body and eel-like movements, it glides amongst the corals in search of prey. Eel blennies can be distinguished from the true blennies by their confluent dorsal, caudal and anal fins, and by the absence of pelvic fins. The peculiar shape of the head, size, the dark ocellus on the gill plate, and the rather distinct pattern are characteristic too. This fish is not well known in Australia and very few specimens have been recorded.

Ocellated eel blenny *(C. subducens)*

Family CALLIONYMIDAE
Common Name Splendid mandarinfish
Scientific Name *Synchiropus splendidus* (Herre), 1927
Habitat Coral reef
Distribution Qld.
Depth Range 10 to 20 metres
Adult Size 10 centimetres
Food Habit Carnivorous
Use Aquarium fish
Occurrence Uncommon

Many of the callionymids are brilliant but none can match the mandarinfishes. They are rather rare in Australian waters, but occur on fringing reefs around northern continental islands and adjacent areas of the Great Barrier Reef. *S. splendidus* lives in sheltered lagoons and generally occur in pairs with the male being a little larger than the female. Those on display in Australian aquariums have all been imported. Splendid mandarinfish inhabit broken coral bottom under cover. *S. picturatus* is known from north Western Australia.

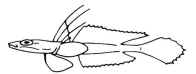

Splendid mandarinfish *(S. splendidus)*

Family GOBIIDAE
Common Name Ocellated goby
Scientific Name *Valenciennea longipinnis* (Lay and Bennett), 1839
Habitat Sand, sandy rubble
Distribution Qld., NT, WA
Depth Range 1 to 10 metres
Adult Size 20 centimetres
Food Habit Carnivorous: worms, crustaceans
Use Aquarium fish
Occurrence Common

One of the larger gobies, *V. longipinnis* has a very beautiful colour pattern. Most of the fish I have observed were in lagoons on broken rubble bottoms dotted by sand patches. The ocellated goby generally occurs in pairs and may be found on mainland reefs, continental reefs and on offshore reefs. Each pair excavate a hole beneath a buried piece of dead coral slab, or a clump of dead coral. During the day they take turns at house cleaning, bringing out pieces of dead coral and mouthfuls of sand and depositing it near the entrance.

Ocellated goby *(V. longipinnis)*

Family GOBIIDAE
Common Name Mural goby
Scientific Name *Valenciennea muralis* (Valenciennes), 1837
Habitat Sand
Distribution Qld., NT, WA
Depth Range 1 to 15 metres
Adult Size 10 centimetres
Food Habit Carnivorous
Use Aquarium fish
Occurrence Common

Mural gobies are almost always seen in pairs. They live around mainland reefs, continental island reefs and along the northern part of the Great Barrier Reef. *V. muralis* selects areas of rather fine sand in lagoons and along the fringes of back reefs; their territorial holes have a wide rim of sand where the gobies have deposited the refuse. The burrow is generally situated in the open.

When feeding, *V. muralis* rarely ventures very far away from its burrow and at the first sign of danger, or an over-anxious underwater photographer, the mural gobies dive into their burrow.

Mural goby *(V. muralis)*

Family GOBIIDAE
Common Name Flasher goby
Scientific Name *Fusigobius* sp. (Gobiid N°35 AMPI)
Habitat Sand
Distribution Qld., WA
Depth Range 5 to 20 metres
Adult Size 10 centimetres
Food Habit Carnivorous
Use Aquarium fish
Occurrence Moderately common

First photographed alive in Western Australia in 1971, the flasher goby was a new record for that State and an undescribed species. It was recorded from the east coast in 1975 and is now known to occur in lagoons and sheltered back reefs along the northern Great Barrier Reef. During the day the flasher goby does not venture out from its territorial cave, or ledge. It selects caves with sandy floors and at night occupies an excavated burrow at the rear, well away from the entrance. The males have a long spine on their dorsal fin that is often erected very quickly, hence the name, flasher goby.

Flasher goby *(Fusigobius* sp.)

Family GOBIIDAE
Common Name Fire goby
Scientific Name *Nemateleotris magnifica* Fowler, 1938
Habitat Coral reef
Distribution Qld.
Depth Range 2 to 25 metres
Adult Size 31 centimetres
Food Habit Carnivorous
Use Aquarium fish
Occurrence Uncommon

Always in a pair, the fire gobies are delicate, little fishes which maintain a head up stance, and rarely sit on the bottom. Instead, they maintain positions close to their burrow a few centimetres to 0.5 metres off the bottom and appear to feed on plankton. With a little care they can be observed at close range. They tend to live on hard bottoms and may be seen around the terraces of large bommies in open water and midway along surge gutters in reef fronts. *N. magnifica* inhabits the outer northern areas of the Great Barrier Reef and in the Coral Sea.

Fire goby *(N. magnifica)*

Family GOBIIDAE
Common Name Four-eyed goby
Scientific Name *Signigobius biocellatus* Hoese and Allen, 1977
Habitat Sand and coral reef
Distribution Qld.
Depth Range 3 to 25 metres
Adult Size 5 centimetres
Food Habit Carnivorous
Use Aquarium fish
Occurrence Uncommon

Only recently described, the four-eyed goby, although small, is one of the most interesting of all gobies. It lives around continental islands and the Great Barrier Reef where it excavates burrows in the sand or on occasions takes over unoccupied burrows of other species. Sometimes they live on open sand amongst broken reef, or on sandy terraces and even in the sandy floors of caves. There is always a male and female together and these may mate for life. These gobies spend a lot of the day excavating their burrow, bringing out mouthfuls of sand and ejecting it to one side. Each goby takes a turn to go below while the other, perched on its large pelvic fins, watches at the entrance.

Four-eyed goby *(S. biocellatus)*

Family GOBIIDAE
Common Name Crossed goby
Scientific Name *Amblygobius decussatus* (Bleeker), 1885
Habitat Sand, coral reef, rubble
Distribution Qld., WA
Depth Range 5 to 15 metres
Adult Size 15 centimetres
Food Habit Carnivorous
Use Aquarium fish
Occurrence Moderately common

Gobies make very good aquarium pets, though they are apt to disturb the settings a little and continually burrow into the substrate. Due to the fact that many sand gobies feed by taking in mouthfuls of sand, ingesting the organic matter and letting the rest pass out through their gills, it is necessary to have sand in the aquarium. Even when they feed on food dropped into the tank, they will still take in sand. The crossed goby lives in sheltered lagoon waters on northern mainland reefs, continental reefs and along the northern end of the Great Barrier Reef. It generally prefers a broken rubble bottom.

Crossed goby *(A. decussatus)*

Family ACANTHURIDAE
Common Name Brown tang
Scientific Name *Zebrasoma scopas* (Cuvier), 1829
Habitat Coral reef, rocky reef
Distribution Qld., WA (also NSW)
Depth Range 2 to 10 metres
Adult Size 20 centimetres
Food Habit Herbivorous: algae
Use Aquarium fish
Occurrence Uncommon

One of the smaller surgeonfish, with a characteristic shape, this species was recorded from Australian waters in the early 1970s. The brown tang is found on mainland reefs, continental island reefs and throughout the Great Barrier Reef. It 'flits' around the coral, staying close to the bottom, in lagoons, and along sheltered back reefs. This little fish is very popular with marine aquarists and is quite hardy.

Brown tang *(Z. scopas)*

Family ACANTHURIDAE
Common Name Sailfin tang
Scientific Name *Zebrasoma veliferum* (Bloch), 1795
Habitat Coral reef, rocky reef
Distribution Qld., WA (also NSW)
Depth Range 2 to 20 metres
Adult Size 40 centimetres
Food Habit Herbivorous: algae
Use Aquarium fish, edible
Occurrence Moderately common

Distinctively marked and shaped, the sailfin tang can be seen alone, as pairs, or in a school. Like most acanthurids they range over a large area feeding on filamentous algae. They live in sheltered lagoons and along the edges of terraced backreefs and are sometimes seen feeding in shallow reef flats as the tide runs in. *Z. veliferum* ranges from mainland reefs onto the outer Great Barrier Reef and pairs often spend a great deal of time chasing each other and displaying their 'sails'. At night they sleep in caves and crevices with their 'sails' erect.

Sailfin tang *(Z. veliferum). Inset: 'sail' displayed*

Family ACANTHURIDAE
Common Name Dussumier's surgeonfish
Scientific Name *Acanthurus dussumieri* Valenciennes, 1835
Habitat Coral reef, rocky reef, rubble
Distribution Qld., NT, WA
Depth Range 5 to 20 metres
Adult Size 40 centimetres
Food Habit Herbivorous: algae
Use Edible
Occurrence Common

Seen singularly or more often in groups and small schools, Dussumier's surgeonfish feed on filamentous algae cropped from coral rubble and sometimes even sand surfaces. It seems to prefer the quieter areas of lagoons and back reefs, though in Western Australia it is commonly observed on open water mainland reefs. Dussumier's surgeonfish is edible, but every care must be taken, if handling this species with bare hands, as the caudal blades may inflict serious wounds.

Dussumier's surgeonfish *(A. dussumieri)*

Family ACANTHURIDAE
Common Name Blue-lined surgeonfish
Scientific Name *Acanthurus lineatus* (Linnaeus), 1758
Habitat Coral reef, rocky reef
Distribution Qld., NT, WA
Depth Range 1 to 8 metres
Adult Size 27 centimetres
Food Habit Herbivorous: algae
Use Edible
Occurrence Common

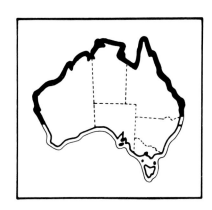

The most beautiful of all the surgeonfish and one of the most common, this species lives on and around the tops of reefs where it maintains a small area of algae-covered reef surrounded by territories of its own kind. *A. lineatus* is a fast swimming surgeonfish which can be seen on continental island reefs where there is moderate current, or water movement around headlands and on the seaward platforms and reef rims. Although attractively coloured, this fish must not be handled alive with bare hands as it has razor sharp extendible blades on the caudal peduncle.

Blue-lined surgeonfish *(A. lineatus)*

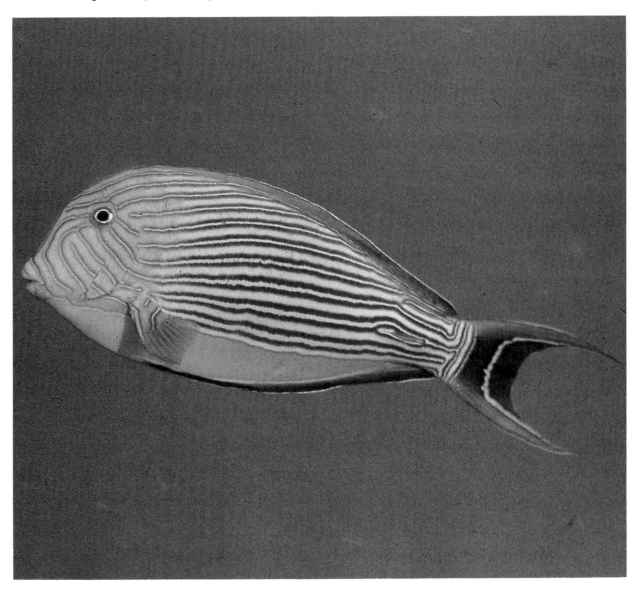

Family ACANTHURIDAE
Common Name Orange-gilled surgeonfish
Scientific Name *Acanthurus pyroferus* Kittlitz, 1834
Habitat Coral reef
Distribution Qld.
Depth Range 3 to 25 metres
Adult Size 25 centimetres
Food Habit Herbivorous: algae
Use Edible
Occurrence Common

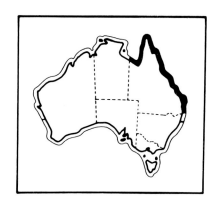

A few surgeonfishes, especially the very dark coloured ones without distinguishing patterns, or markings, are difficult to identify underwater. *A. pyroferus* can be almost black all over, but has an orange patch near the gill, a white line around its nose and a bright orange, or yellow edged lunate tail. The orange-gilled surgeonfish is found along the northern Great Barrier Reef and inhabits terraces and channel slopes below the reef rim, in lagoons and along back reefs. It is a fast elusive swimmer that has a pair of sharp caudal blades.

Orange-gilled surgeonfish *(A. pyroferus)*

Family ACANTHURIDAE
Common Name White-cheeked surgeonfish
Scientific Name *Acanthurus glaucopareius* Cuvier, 1829
Habitat Coral reef
Distribution Qld., WA
Depth Range 2 to 10 metres
Adult Size 27 centimetres
Food Habit Herbivorous: algae
Use Aquarium fish
Occurrence Uncommon

Beautiful, and elusive, the white-cheeked surgeonfish is a solitary, territorial fish which occupies small areas on the tops of submerged reefs, where there is a profusion of coral growth. Most abundant on the northern outer Great Barrier Reef and Coral Sea. *A. glaucopareius* is easily identified by the white band on the snout and the white half-moon beneath the eye. Though fairly simple to get close to, the white-cheeked surgeonfish is difficult to photograph, as it is always on the move and lives in strong currents. Care must be taken when handling this fish due to its sharp caudal blades.

White-cheeked surgeonfish *(A. glaucopareius)*

Family ACANTHURIDAE
Common Name Thompson's surgeonfish
Scientific Name *Acanthurus thompsoni* (Fowler), 1923
Habitat Coral reef
Distribution
Depth Range 8 to 25 metres
Adult Size 20 centimetres
Food Habit Carnivorous: zooplankton
Use Aquarium fish
Occurrence Uncommon

A relatively small member of the family *Acanthuridae*, this species has only been recently sighted on the northern off-shore reefs of the Great Barrier Reef. Thompson's surgeonfish is known to occur in schools in other Pacific areas, but as yet I have only observed individuals. Colour does not vary much, the body is bluish-grey to black, the tail is lunate and a startling white. There is a distinct black spot just below the posterior end of the dorsal fin, above the caudal peduncle. This species may be seen on reef fronts and also in behind back reefs, close to deep channels, where it feeds.

Thompson's surgeonfish *(A. thompsoni)*

Family ACANTHURIDAE
Common Name Longnose unicornfish
Scientific Name *Naso unicornis* (Forsskål), 1775
Habitat Coral reef
Distribution Qld., WA
Depth Range 10 to 30 metres
Adult Size 55 centimetres
Food Habit Herbivorous: algae
Use Edible
Occurrence Common

N. unicornis is very easy to identify as an adult due to its colour, shape of its horn and the two bright blue fixed keels on the caudal peduncle. Sometimes seen alone and other times in small groups, the longnose unicornfish is difficult to get close to underwater, though it is often speared. This species feeds primarily on algae which it takes from around bommies and dead reef surfaces. Juveniles do not begin to form a horn until they are around 12 centimetres, when there is a small bump present on the forehead in the vicinity of the eye. Rarely line caught, it is quite edible. The blue keels may inflict wounds if the fish is held alive.

Longnose unicornfish *(N. unicornis)*

Family ACANTHURIDAE
Common Name Hump-head unicornfish
Scientific Name *Naso tuberosus* Lacépède, 1802
Habitat Coral reef
Distribution Qld., WA
Depth Range 8 to 30 metres
Adult Size 60 centimetres
Food Habit Omnivorous
Use Edible
Occurrence Moderately common

Usually sighted at a distance swimming 'hell for leather' in the opposite direction, the hump-head unicornfish is a very difficult fish to approach underwater and most are high off the bottom. This species occurs on reef fronts and in deepwater channels leading through the seaward platforms of the outer and inner Great Barrier Reef and the Coral Sea. *N. tuberosus* may be observed alone in small groups, or more rarely in huge schools. There are two immobile, recurved keels on the caudal peduncle, although they are not as sharp as in the genus *Acanthurus*.

Hump-head unicornfish *(N. tuberosus)*

258

Family ACANTHURIDAE
Common Name Clown unicornfish
Scientific Name *Naso lituratus* (Bloch and Schneider), 1801
Habitat Coral reef, rocky reef
Distribution Qld., NT, WA
Depth Range 2 to 25 metres
Adult Size 50 centimetres
Food Habit Herbivorous: algae
Use Aquarium fish, edible
Occurrence Common

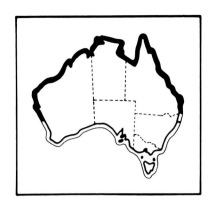

Difficult to get close to underwater, the clown unicornfish is generally a solitary species which lives around continental island reefs and is also frequently sighted on the northern Great Barrier Reef. A very easy fish to identify, it has a pair of thorn-like projections on the caudal peduncle and similar to other members of this family, is capable of causing injury if held in the hand. The male clown unicornfish has a long filament at the top and bottom of the tail. This fish inhabits reef front and lagoon areas, and in shallow water is territorial, having a special crevice in the reef it occupies to retreat to if harassed.

Clown unicornfish *(N. lituratus)*

Family ZANCLIDAE
Common Name Moorish idol
Scientific Name *Zanclus cornutus* Linnaeus, 1758
Habitat Coral reef, rocky reef
Distribution Qld., NT, WA (also NSW)
Depth Range 2 to 25 metres
Adult Size 22 centimetres
Food Habit Carnivorous: encrusting sessile invertebrates
Use Aquarium fish
Occurrence Common

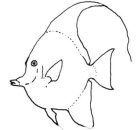

Sometimes referred to as *Z. canescens*, this name was applied to the juveniles of *Z. cornutus* and is not now recognised. *Z. cornutus* is related to the surgeonfish but lacks the blades on the caudal peduncle. It can be seen alone, in pairs, or small groups. On occasion this species is known to form huge schools and it is thought this may be a prelude to spawning. Moorish idols are the only representative of their family and due to their unique shape are easy to identify. Underwater they can be approached without difficulty as they swim slowly around searching for the small sponges they feed on.

Moorish idol *(Z. cornutus)*

Family SIGANIDAE
Common Name Blue-lined rabbitfish
Scientific Name *Siganus puellus* (Schlegel), 1852
Habitat Coral reef, rocky reef
Distribution Qld.
Depth Range 5 to 20 metres
Adult Size 30 centimetres
Food Habit Herbivorous: algae
Use Edible
Occurrence Uncommon

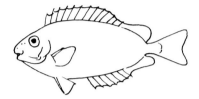

Rabbitfishes are rarely caught by line, though many are netted and some are speared. Their flesh, although edible, has a definite weedy taste, and the fish should be cleaned and skinned immediately on capture. Properly prepared and served with some seasoning they are quite acceptable. The blue-lined rabbitfish inhabit lagoons along the Great Barrier Reef and are more common in the northern reaches. They also live around mainland reefs and continental islands. Similar to most rabbitfish, *S. puellus* is often sighted in pairs which are not always easy to approach underwater. This fish should never be handled without adequate protection as it has a number of venomous spines.

Blue-lined rabbitfish *(S. puellus)*

Family SIGANIDAE
Common Name Gold-spotted rabbitfish
Scientific Name *Siganus punctatus* Bloch and Schneider, 1801
Habitat Coral reef
Distribution Qld.
Depth Range 5 to 20 metres
Adult Size 38 centimetres
Food Habit Herbivorous: algae
Use Edible
Occurrence Uncommon

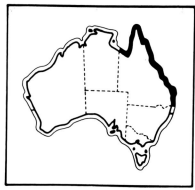

The gold-spoted rabbitfish is almost always observed in pairs swimming close together over many hundreds of metres of reef, feeding exclusively on algae from dead coral surfaces and the walls of cliff faces. It is found throughout the Great Barrier Reef and continental islands but is most abundant around the offshore reefs and cays. This species should not be handled carelessly as it has sharp venomous spines. The flesh has a weedy taste but it is *not* poisonous.

Gold-spotted rabbitfish *(S. punctatus)*

Family SIGANIDAE
Common Name Golden-lined rabbitfish
Scientific Name *Siganus lineatus* (Valenciennes), 1835
Habitat Coral reef, rocky reef
Distribution Qld., NT, WA
Depth Range 2 to 20 metres
Adult Size 35 centimetres
Food Habit Herbivorous: algae
Use Edible
Occurrence Common

Sometimes occurring in large schools which enter the surge channels of open water reefs around continental islands, *S. lineatus* also inhabits sheltered mainland reefs and lagoons along the Great Barrier Reef. The golden-lined rabbitfish is one of the largest and most gaily coloured rabbitfish and can be readily identified by the bright golden lines and the yellow spot at the rear of the dorsal fin. It is a diurnal herbivore which varies little in its colour pattern. The flesh is edible, though requiring some preparation and added condiments. This fish should be handled carefully as it has venomous spines.

Golden-lined rabbitfish *(S. lineatus)*

Family SIGANIDAE
Common Name Fuscous rabbitfish
Scientific Name *Siganus fuscescens* (Houttuyn), 1872
Habitat Coral reef, rocky reef
Distribution Qld., NT
Depth Range 1 to 20 metres
Adult Size 35 centimetres
Food Habit Herbivorous: algae, plankton
Use Edible
Occurrence Common

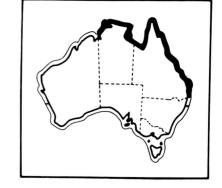

Fuscous rabbitfish are rather nonedescript in colour with a grey back, silvery undersides and a faint yellow blotch on the head between the eyes; the back has multitudes of small white spots. *S. fuscuscens* swim in small groups or in schools, spending a lot of its time above the reef, and has been observed to bite at passing plankton. This fish lives behind the reef proper and usually feeds on algae growing on broken coral rubble and sand similar to some acanthurids with which the fuscous rabbitfish often feeds. The flesh of *S. fuscescens*, although edible, is somewhat lacking in quality. The venom in the spines is quite potent.

Fuscous rabbitfish *(S. fuscescens)*

Family SIGANIDAE
Common Name Black-face rabbitfish
Scientific Name *Siganus vulpinus* Slager & Muller, 1844
Habitat Coral reef
Distribution Qld.
Depth Range 5 to 20 metres
Adult Size 20 centimetres
Food Habit Omnivorous: algae, sessile organisms
Use Edible
Occurrence Moderately common

Looking like a butterflyfish, this species was for many years known under the generic name *Lo*. The velvet-black face, long snout and bright yellow body make it an outstanding sight amongst the corals. *S. vulpinus* occurs throughout the Great Barrier Reef and is almost always seen in pairs. It is extremely difficult to approach as it invariably swims out on open reefs and picks amongst the growths whilst swimming. The black-face rabbitfish roam over large areas in lagoons and around back reefs.

Black-face rabbitfish *(S. vulpinus)*

Family SIGANIDAE
Common Name Barred rabbitfish
Scientific Name *Siganus doliatus* (Valenciennes), 1835
Habitat Coral reef, rocky reef
Distribution Qld., WA
Depth Range 2 to 20 metres
Adult Size 30 centimetres
Food Habit Herbivorous: algae
Use Edible
Occurrence Common

At a distance, the barred rabbitfish can be confused with *S. puellus* as their colours and patterns are somewhat similar. Although the normal body colour of *S. doliatus* is brown, the fish shown here is lighter in colour due to it being cleaned. The blue-lined rabbitfish has only one black bar crossing from the top of the head through the eye to the lower jaw. On *S. doliatus* there are two dark bars, one from the eye to the lower jaw and a much larger one running parallel to it across the back and under the gill plates. This fish has venomous spines and the flesh is of poor quality.

Barred rabbitfish *(S. doliatus)*

Family SCOMBRIDAE
Common Name Narrow-barred Spanish mackerel
Scientific Name *Scomberomorus commerson* (Lacépède), 1880
Habitat Open sea, coral reef, rocky reef
Distribution Qld., NT, WA
Depth Range Surface to 30 metres
Adult Size 2.5 metres
Food Habit Carnivorous: fish
Use Edible
Occurrence Common

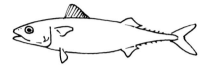

A well-known commercial fish, narrow-barred Spanish mackerel are trolled around mainland islands off north-western Australia and Great Barrier Reef islands, cays and bommies off the Queensland coast. Although they are seen underwater, this fast swimming species remains near the surface in open water around the edges of reefs. The narrow-barred Spanish mackerel feed voraciously on surface schooling fishes. They are caught by trolling outriggers, handlines, and rods using fish bait, or spoons and are very good to eat.

Narrow-barred Spanish mackerel *(S. commerson)*

Family SCOMBRIDAE
Common Name Shark mackerel
Scientific Name *Grammatorcynus bicarinatus* (Quoy and Gaimard), 1825
Habitat Open water, coral reef, rocky reef
Distribution Qld., NT, WA
Depth Range 8 to 30 metres
Adult Size 1 metre
Food Habit Carnivorous: fish
Use Edible
Occurrence Common

Common inshore and offshore, around the entire north coast, the shark mackerel is found throughout the entire Great Barrier Reef system. Small fish may be seen in schools but most observations are on lone fish which patrol along the reef edges at around 5 to 10 metres. They are caught on outriggers, rods and trolled handlines, using small surface fishes and spoons. The double lateral line makes this fish easy to recognise. Its common name is derived from its shark-like smell when cleaned. This fish makes good eating provided it is bled on capture and cleaned as soon as possible. I like it grilled.

Shark mackerel *(G. bicarinatus)*

Family SCOMBRIDAE
Common Name Dogtooth tuna
Scientific Name *Gymnosarda unicolor* (Rüppell), 1838
Habitat Open sea, coral reef
Distribution Qld.
Depth Range 10 to 45 metres
Adult Size 1.5 metres
Food Habit Carnivorous: fish, squid
Use Edible
Occurrence Moderatey common

Regularly seen by divers on the outer Great Barrier Reef and Coral Sea, dogtooth tuna are powerful predators, swimming in small groups. They tend to be wary, yet very inquisitive as they will swim around a diver at a distance of several metres. This fish has quite large teeth which can be seen in the jaws even at a distance underwater. It can be caught by line and is sometimes trolled by marlin fishermen in northern waters. The flesh is white and quite palatable.

Dogtooth tuna *(G. unicolor)*

Family SCOMBRIDAE
Common Name Rake-gilled mackerel
Scientific Name *Rastrelliger kanagurta* (Cuvier), 1817
Habitat Open sea
Distribution Qld., NT, WA (also NSW)
Depth Range Surface to 10 metres
Adult Size 27 centimetres
Food Habit Carnivorous: crustaceans
Use Edible
Occurrence Uncommon

This fish can be distinguished by the greenish-blue spots and broken
wavy lines on the back that blend into three or four stripes along the
sides. There is also a black spot on the base of the pectoral fin. There
are few schooling scombrids that will tolerate a wetsuited diver at
close range. I have observed *R. kanagurta*, however, feeding along the
edge of a deep drop-off just before dusk. Swimming past in a tightly
packed school they appear to detect masses of shrimp-like
crustaceans which they strain from the water by using their gillrakers.
This species is a fair table fish that often ends up as bait.

Rake-gilled mackerel *(R. kanagurta)*

Family BOTHIDAE
Common Name Leopard flounder
Scientific Name *Bothus pantherinus* (Rüppell), 1828
Habitat Sand
Distribution Qld. (also NSW)
Depth Range 1 to 30 metres
Adult Size 23 centimetres
Food Habit Carnivorous: crustaceans
Use Edible
Occurrence Common

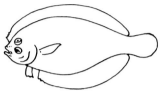

Far more numerous than most divers would imagine, the leopard flounder can be handlined, trawled, or seined, on mainland and offshore sandy, or sandy mud bottom. Similar to other members of this family, *B. pantherinus* can alter its colouration to match its surroundings, however, its body pattern can be detected whether it is on dark or light substrate. The leopard flounder is a diurnal predator that hides beneath the sand with only its telescopic eyes showing above the surface. These eyes are able to see in all directions and can pick up any disturbance in the sand caused by buried prey. A very attractive species it is covered with blue-edged ocelli and a conspicuous large black crest on the lateral line, towards the tail.

Leopard flounder *(B. pantherinus)*

Family BOTHIDAE
Common Name Spiny-headed flounder
Scientific Name *Engyprosodon grandisquamma* (Schlegel), 1846
Habitat Sand
Distribution Qld., WA, NT (also NSW)
Depth Range 6 to 35 metres
Adult Size 20 centimetres
Food Habit Carnivorous: crustaceans
Use Edible
Occurrence Moderately common

Commonly trawled on coarse sand and gravel bottom, with a colour pattern almost identical to the substrate, this little flounder is almost impossible to see. It can be readily identified by the black spot on either side of its tail and the prominent ocelli along the junction of the dorsal and anal fins. Although small, there is no reason why a number wouldn't make good fish soup.

Spiny-headed flounder *(E. grandisquamma)*

Family SOLEIDAE
Common Name Peacock sole
Scientific Name *Achirus pavoninus* (Lacépède), 1802
Habitat Sand
Distribution Qld., NT, WA
Depth Range 4 to 20 metres
Adult Size 23 centimetres
Food Habit Carnivorous: crustaceans
Use Edible
Occurrence Common

A beautifully marked fish, the peacock sole spends most of its time beneath a layer of sand ambushing prey and hiding from predators; only its eyes betray its presence. All soles of the genus *Achirus* have tails that are separate from the side fins. The eyes are on the right side of the head and there are open pores at the base of each fin ray. These pores release a predator inhibiting secretion which may be useful as a shark repellent. However, as this species is not collected in large numbers a closely related species, Hedley's peacock sole (see *Australian Sea Fishes South 30°S*) was chosen for experiments overseas.

Peacock sole *(A. pavoninus)*

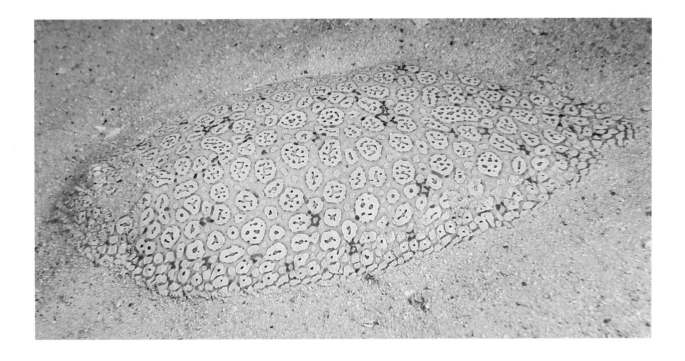

Family BALISTIDAE
Common Name Clown triggerfish
Scientific Name *Balistoides conspicillus* (Bloch and Schneider), 1801
Habitat Coral reef
Distribution Qld., NT (also NSW)
Depth Range 3 to 30 metres
Adult Size 35 centimetres
Food Habit Carnivorous: invertebrates, molluscs
Use Aquarium fish
Occurrence Uncommon

This brilliantly coloured, much sought after aquarium fish can be seen in the shallows of lagoons, or at depth around terraced reef fronts on the outer Great Barrier Reef. The clown triggerfish is generally territorial and is almost always seen alone. It is not easy to get close to and when pursued holes up, or flees out of sight. Triggerfish need careful handling as they have strong sharp teeth and will bite anything in reach. They are suspected of being poisonous.

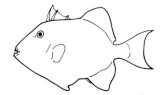

Clown triggerfish *(B. conspicillus)*

Family BALISTIDAE
Common Name Vermiculated triggerfish
Scientific Name *Balistapus undulatus* (Park), 1797
Habitat Coral reef
Distribution Qld.
Depth Range 5 to 25 metres
Adult Size 35 centimetres
Food Habit Omnivorous
Use Aquarium fish
Occurrence Uncommon

A fast-swimming, very distinctive species *B. undulatus* inhabits back reefs, channel slopes, bommies and reef front terraces adjacent to drop-offs. This fish occurs throughout the Great Barrier Reef, but is more prevalent towards the northern extremities. It is most difficult to get close to underwater and takes refuge in the nearest hole or beneath coral at the slightest hint of danger. It is territorial and usually seen alone. Small specimens make good aquarium pets. Larger fish should not be eaten as they are believed to be poisonous.

Vermiculated triggerfish *(B. undulatus)*

Family BALISTIDAE
Common Name Eye-stripe triggerfish
Scientific Name *Sufflamen chrysopterus* (Bloch and Schneider), 1801
Habitat Coral reef, rubble
Distribution Qld., NT, WA
Depth Range 3 to 20 metres
Adult Size 22 centimetres
Food Habit Carnivorous: molluscs, worms, echinoderms
Use Aquarium fish
Occurrence Common

Though the eye-stripe triggerfish varies in colour throughout its distribution, from light brown to dark brown, the stripe below its eye is always present. *S. chrysopterus* is a territorial triggerfish which inhabits sheltered back reefs and lagoons on the mainland, around continental islands and throughout the Great Barrier Reef. Within its territory there are generally one or two coral clumps which have escape holes. When approached closely the eye-stripe triggerfish dives into the closest hole, bites onto a piece of coral and locks its dorsal spine into place. Short of demolishing the coral clump nothing will remove it.

Eye-stripe triggerfish *(S. chrysopterus)*

Family MONACANTHIDAE
Common Name Red-tail leatherjacket
Scientific Name *Pervagor melanocephalus* (Bleeker), 1853
Habitat Coral reef
Distribution Qld. (also NSW)
Depth Range 1 to 15 metres
Adult Size 12 centimetres
Food Habit Omnivorous: algae, coral polyps
Use Aquarium fish
Occurrence Uncommon

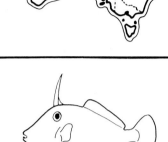

The red-tail leatherjacket's dark colour and very shy behaviour makes it a very difficult species to photograph. This cryptic little fish can be found in sheltered lagoons throughout the Great Barrier Reef and around bommies and back reefs of the Coral Sea. Some specimens may appear to be all black but the orange, or yellow ring around the eye is fairly constant. When feeding, it picks at a variety of encrusting organisms, including coral polyps and algae.

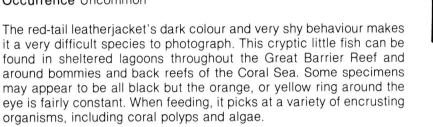

Red-tail leatherjacket *(P. melanocephalus)*

Family MONACANTHIDAE
Common Name Scribbled leatherjacket
Scientific Name *Alutera scripta* (Osbeck), 1765
Habitat Coral reef, rocky reef
Distribution Qld., NT (also NSW)
Depth Range 2 to 25 metres
Adult Size 1.2 metres
Food Habit Omnivorous
Use Poisonous
Occurrence Common

The scribbled leatherjacket is the largest of its family in Australia and one of the most ornamental. With such a distinct shape and colour pattern it is quite easy to identify and even when dead still retains some of its colour pattern. This solitary species inhabits shallow water lagoons and the rich coral slopes of back reefs, usually in sheltered water. One specimen was seen on the outer reef edge on the Great Barrier Reef. The scribbled leatherjacket ranges over a wide area of reef and is a rather shy fish. *A. scripta* is reported as being poisonous in some areas.

Scribbled leatherjacket *(A. scripta)*

Family MONACANTHIDAE
Common Name Large-scaled leatherjacket
Scientific Name *Cantheschenia grandisquamis* Hutchins, 1977
Habitat Coral reef, rocky reef
Distribution Qld.
Depth Range 5 to 30 metres
Adult Size 18 centimetres
Food Habit Carnivorous: molluscs, echinoderms
Use Edible
Occurrence Uncommon

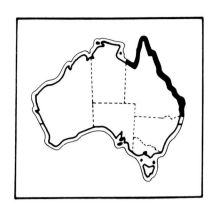

Although I photographed this species in 1969, it was not described until 1977. Known only from the east coast it is found on fringing reefs around continental islands, and throughout the Great Barrier Reef on back reefs and on the slopes of reefs adjacent to channels. During summer pairs may be observed; in winter the fish appear to be solitary. This fish may be caught by line and is as succulent as any of the larger leatherjackets.

Large-scaled leatherjacket *(C. grandisquamis)*, male

Family MONACANTHIDAE
Common Name Dumeril's leatherjacket
Scientific Name *Cantherhines dumerili* (Hollard), 1854
Habitat Coral reef, rocky reef
Distribution Qld. (also NSW)
Depth Range 5 to 25 metres
Adult Size 30 centimetres
Food Habit Carnivorous: corals
Use Edible
Occurrence Uncommon

This species is by far the most elusive of all the leatherjackets I have ever photographed. Whereas others are shy and slip away when you are only a few metres from them, *C. dumerili* takes off in a panic 10 to 20 metres away. Adult fish are brownish-yellow with white vertical bands that fade soon after death on the lower half of the body towards the tail. The caudal peduncle has two pairs of forward curving spines. This leatherjacket often swims on its side along the bottom, especially when going away.

Dumeril's leatherjacket *(C. dumerili)*

Family MONACANTHIDAE
Common Name Beaked leatherjacket
Scientific Name *Oxymonacanthus longirostris* (Bloch and Schneider), 1801
Habitat Coral reef, rocky reef
Distribution Qld., NT, WA
Depth Range 1 to 10 metres
Adult Size 8 centimetres
Food Habit Carnivorous: coral polyps
Use Aquarium fish
Occurrence Moderately common

Due to its small size and unobtrusive habits, this fish is generally overlooked by divers. The highly attractive beaked leatherjacket occurs in sheltered lagoons, and on the northwest coast can be seen in the shallows only a few metres out from the mainland. On the east coast it inhabits rich coral areas all along the Great Barrier Reef and fringing reefs around continental islands. Usually in pairs, or small groups it is normally associated with staghorn corals, upon which it feeds.

Beaked leatherjacket *(O. longirostris)*

Family MONACANTHIDAE
Common Name Ribbon leatherjacket
Scientific Name *Anacanthus barbatus* Gray, 1831
Habitat Coral reef, rocky reef, sand, rubble, surface waters
Distribution Qld., NT, WA
Depth Range Surface to 20 metres
Adult Size 25 centimetres
Food Habit Carnivorous
Use Aquarium fish
Occurrence Uncommon

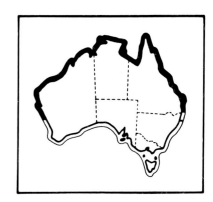

This very distinctive species occupies a wider range of habitats than any other leatherjacket, and when young, swims alongside floating objects on the surface. Unless one is very observant its rather unusual behaviour and cryptic colour pattern makes the ribbon leatherjacket very difficult to find. *A. barbatus* has a tail one-third as long as its body, and a long chin barbel. It is often associated with bottom growths where it adopts a head down position. It is very frequently captured by trawlers working northern prawn grounds.

Ribbon leatherjacket *(A. barbatus)*

Family OSTRACIONTIDAE
Common Name Long-nosed boxfish
Scientific Name *Rhynchostracion nasus* (Bloch), 1785
Habitat Rocky reef, coral reef
Distribution Qld., NT, WA (also NSW)
Depth Range 2 to 20 metres
Adult Size 20 centimetres
Food Habit Omnivorous
Use Aquarium fish
Occurrence Common

The long-nosed boxfish is far more common on coastal reefs and islands than it is on coral cays and reefs along the outer Great Barrier Reef. The fish is generally solitary and quite active during the day. Its white body colour is sometimes yellow and the black spots vary in size. Due to its poor swimming abilities *R. nasus* is very frequently washed up on mainland shores during storms. It is regularly trawled and taken in seine nets. This fish is poisonous.

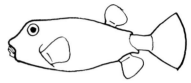

Long-nosed boxfish *(R. nasus)*

Family OSTRACIONTIDAE
Common Name Spotted boxfish
Scientific Name *Ostracion meleagris* Shaw, 1796
Habitat Coral reef, rocky reef
Distribution Qld., NT, WA (also NSW)
Depth Range 3 to 20 metres
Adult Size 22 centimetres
Food Habit Omnivorous: sessile invertebrates, sponges, algae
Use Aquarium fish
Occurrence Uncommon

Some boxfishes are extraordinarily beautiful and *O. meleagris* is no exception; even the female is attractively coloured. Sometimes seen in sheltered lagoons and back reefs along the Great Barrier Reef, the spotted boxfish are more numerous on the inshore lagoon reefs off north-Western Australia. It feeds on a variety of organisms and is always easy to approach. Spotted boxfish are poisonous, and when threatened release a highly toxic substance into the water. They are popular aquarium fish but need a tank to themselves.

Spotted boxfish *(O. meleagris)*

Family TETRAODONTIDAE
Common Name Starry pufferfish
Scientific Name *Arothron stellatus* (Bloch and Schneider), 1875-8
Habitat Rocky reef, coral reef
Distribution Qld., NT, WA (also NSW)
Depth Range 8 to 25 metres
Adult Size 1 metre
Food Habit Omnivorous: echinoderms, molluscs, algae
Use Aquarium fish (juvenile)
Occurrence Common

Arothron stellatus is a large pufferfish which spends all but the early morning and late afternoon curled up in a cave or sheltering beneath a ledge. The starry pufferfish is omnivorous and will eat algae, echinoderms, worms, molluscs, crustaceans and ascidians. It is often trawled and can be caught by line. Care should be taken when handling this fish for its strong jaws and sharp, fused, parrot-like teeth can amputate a finger, or chop out a piece of flesh. This fish is poisonous.

Starry pufferfish *(A. stellatus)*

Family TETRAODONTIDAE
Common Name Scribbled pufferfish
Scientific Name *Arothron mappa* (Lesson), 1830
Habitat Coral reef
Distribution Qld.
Depth Range 5 to 25 metres
Adult Size 30 centimetres
Food Habit Omnivorous: algae, ascidians, molluscs, echinoderms
Use Of no use
Occurrence Uncommon

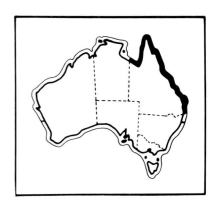

A rather rare pufferfish *A. mappa* is found throughout the entire Great Barrier Reef. Unless the fish is surprised, or driven into its retreat after early morning feeding, it is not easily approached. The scribbled pufferfish inhabits coral lagoons and back reefs and feeds on algae, molluscs, echinoderms and ascidians. At night, it sleeps beneath a ledge in a curled-tail position and turns very light in colour. The flesh of *A. mappa* is deadly poisonous.

Scribbled pufferfish *(A. mappa)*

Family TETRAODONTIDAE
Common Name Narrow-lined pufferfish
Scientific Name *Arothron immaculatus* (Bloch and Schneider), 1801
Habitat Coral reef, rocky reef
Distribution Qld., NT, WA (also NSW)
Depth Range 1 to 20 metres
Adult Size 30 centimetres
Food Habit Omnivorous
Use Of no use
Occurrence Common

The narrow-lined pufferfish is fairly common on mainland reefs and in estuaries, where it is trawled, seined or caught on handlines. It is rare on the Great Barrier Reef but is found around many of the continental islands. *A. immaculatus* is easily approached underwater and is often in the open, or beneath high ledges during the day. This species seems to be territorial in behaviour. It is highly poisonous.

Narrow-lined pufferfish *(A. immaculatus)*

Family TETRAODONTIDAE
Common Name Valentin's sharpnose pufferfish
Scientific Name *Canthigaster valentini* (Bleeker), 1829
Habitat Coral reef, rocky reef
Distribution Qld. (also NSW)
Depth Range 1 to 30 metres
Adult Size 7 centimetres
Food Habit Omnivorous
Use Aquarium fish
Occurrence Common

Valentin's sharpnose pufferfish is common along the Great Barrier Reef on mainland reefs, and around continental islands. This fish is mimicked by the small leatherjacket *Paraluteres prionurus* which is almost identical in colouration and swims in a similar fashion. They are easily separated, as the Valentin's sharpnose puffer has no dorsal spine, no thorn-like spines on the caudal peduncle and has fewer dorsal and anal rays. Both fishes have a shy and retiring behaviour; *C. valentini* is far more common than its mimic.

Valentin's sharpnose pufferfish *(C. valentini)*

Family TETRAODONTIDAE
Common Name Banded sharpnose pufferfish
Scientific Name *Canthigaster coronata* (Vaillant and Sauvage), 1875
Habitat Coral reef
Distribution Qld., WA (also NSW)
Depth Range 3 to 20 metres
Adult Size 10 centimetres
Food Habit Omnivorous: algae, crustaceans
Use Aquarium fish
Occurrence Uncommon

There are around nine species of sharpnose pufferfish so far recorded from Australian waters; some have been known for many years whilst others have been recorded just recently. Some of these new records are due to sightings, photographs and specimens from underwater naturalists and others from collections made by marine biologists. *C. coronata* lives along the Great Barrier Reef, on mainland reefs in north-Western Australia, and in the Coral Sea. It prefers sheltered conditions and feeds on a variety of organisms, including algae, crustaceans, worms, sponges and molluscs.

Banded sharpnose pufferfish *(C. coronata)*

Family TETRAODONTIDAE
Common Name Solandri's sharpnose pufferfish
Scientific Name *Canthigaster solandri* (Richardson), 1844
Habitat Coral reef, rocky reef
Distribution Qld. (also NSW)
Depth Range 5 to 20 metres
Adult Size 12 centimetres
Food Habit Omnivorous: coraline algae, ascidians, molluscs
Use Aquarium fish
Occurrence Uncommon

Most sharpnose pufferfish inhabit shallow sheltered waters and each species has a definite colour pattern. Solandri's sharpnose pufferfish normally has very prominent light blue lines and specks, but in some specimens these are less conspicuous and appear much darker. The red ring around the eye and the black ocellus directly beneath the dorsal fin are characteristic features. *C. solandri* is an interesting and unusual aquarium fish which is easily maintained.

Solandri's sharpnose pufferfish *(C. solandri)*

Family DIODONTIDAE
Common Name Freckled porcupinefish
Scientific Name *Diodon holacanthus* Linnaeus, 1758
Habitat Coral reef, rocky reef
Distribution Qld., NT, WA (also NSW)
Depth Range 1 to 25 metres
Adult Size 50 centimetres
Food Habit Carnivorous: molluscs, crustaceans
Use Curiosity
Occurrence Common

This fish may be found sleeping in a curve-tailed position amongst bottom growths, under ledges, or in rock fissures during the day. It hardly moves when touched but becomes active at night when it feeds. When asleep its colours remain unchanged, which is unusual, as most fish have a different colour pattern for day and night. The freckled porcupinefish is poisonous to eat. If caught on a line it is best to cut it off, as the teeth can cause injury.

Freckled porcupinefish (*D. holacanthus*)

INDEX

ABOUT THE AUTHOR

NEVILLE COLEMAN was born near the shores of the Lane Cove River in Sydney. As he grew up, fishing became his all-consuming occupation; at ten years of age his most ardent aspirations were to become an explorer or a pirate – preferably both.

On leaving school he completed an apprenticeship in photo-lithography and became familiar with all facets of photographic reproduction. His life reached a major turning point in 1963 when, drawn by a love of nature and an unquenchable thirst for knowledge, he began to spend his spare time diving in Sydney's harbour and coastal waters, finding many rare and beautiful marine animals. He dreamed constantly of discovery and felt a great desire to explore, to seek and to find what had never been found. After two years of preparation he conducted the *Australian Coastal Marine Expedition,* a total of almost four years travelling 64,000 kilometres around Australia observing, recording, photographing and collecting many thousands of marine creatures. This was the first photographic subtidal survey every attempted on an Australia-wide basis.

Since 1973, Neville has cross-referenced approximately 40,000 transparencies of marine animals and plants. The *Australasian Marine Photographic Index* of which he is curator, is the largest scientifically-curated indentification system in the Southern Hemisphere.

During recent years he has also taken part in or organised 20 smaller expeditions to various parts of Australasia, written 20 authoritative books on Australian marine life, supplied articles to over 30 magazines throughout the world and had photographs published in 65 books, including some produced by the National Geographic Society and Time-Life. Many of his photographs are on permanent display at the Australian Museum and the National Museum of Victoria.

Neville and his work have made successful inroads into the medium of television with a 30-minute documentary for ITV's *Nature Watch* filmed in Papua New Guinea and shown in England, Scotland and New Zealand with substantial ratings.

The ABC *Big Country* programme took Neville to Lord Howe Island to film *Akin to the Sea* and he has appeared in *Simon Townsend's Wonderworld, Earthwatch, Good Morning Sydney, The Mike Walsh Show,* and on many talkback radio sessions.

His photographic exhibitions have been shown extensively throughout eastern Australia and he lectures regularly in Australia, Papua New Guinea and New Zealand.

More recently, Neville has produced for the first time in Australia, a high-quality journal based on education and conservation of the sea. This glossy quarterly appropriately named *Underwater, the Challenge of Tomorrow* has already established itself as an authority in its field.

An associate of the Australian Museum, Neville is recognised as Australasia's leading underwater Naturalist. In 20 years of exploring and recording the Underwater World, Neville has logged over 10,000 dives, found and photographed over 10,000 species of aquatic animals and plants, discovering 200 new species – many of which now bear his name.

In this book he has drawn from a lifetime of dedication, his experiences on trawlers: charter, game and cruise boats; research vessels; cray boats, and gill netters. He has also notched up thousands of handlining hours, and had vast experience beneath the sea. In ten thousand dives logged over twenty years, Neville has achieved what may seem to most an incredible accomplishment.

He has taken the dreams of a ten-year-old and made them come true.

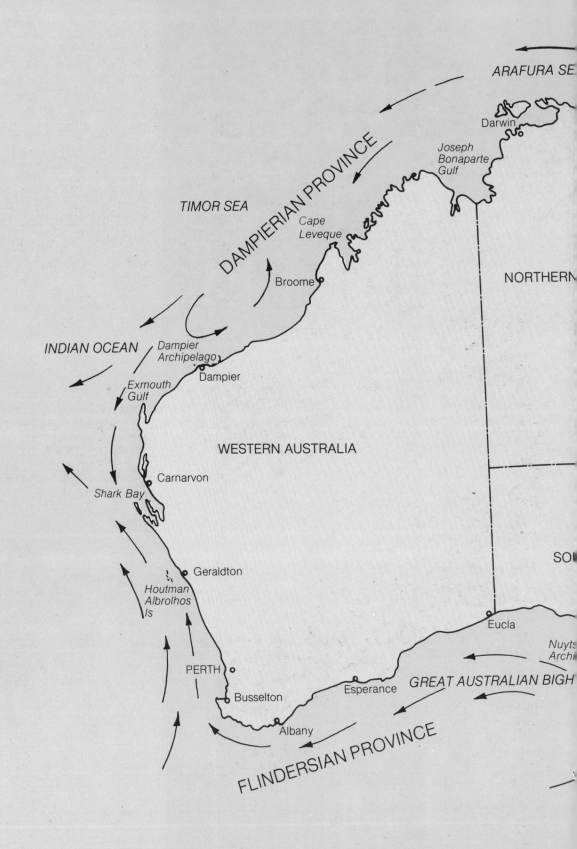

ARAFURA SEA

Darwin

Joseph
Bonaparte
Gulf

NORTHERN

DAMPIERIAN PROVINCE

TIMOR SEA

Cape
Leveque

Broome

INDIAN OCEAN

Dampier
Archipelago

Dampier

Exmouth
Gulf

WESTERN AUSTRALIA

Carnarvon

Shark Bay

SOU

Geraldton

Houtman
Albrolhos
Is

Eucla

Nuyts
Archi

PERTH

GREAT AUSTRALIAN BIGH

Busselton

Esperance

Albany

FLINDERSIAN PROVINCE